The 24-Hour Western Story with ChatGPT

Andrew Parry

Published by Andrew Parry, 2025.

THE 24-HOUR WESTERN STORY WITH CHATGPT

First edition. April 14, 2025.

ISBN: 979-8230866190

Written by Andrew Parry.

Table of Contents

Dreaming of the Frontier: Where Western Stories Begin

Every Western story begins in the same place—not on a dusty trail or in a saloon filled with cigar smoke—but in the imagination. Before you write your first line of dialogue or describe a cowboy silhouetted against the setting sun, you need to tap into the dream of the frontier. The Western genre is more than a setting, more than cowboys and shootouts. It's a mythic space, a romantic vision of freedom, danger, isolation, and the eternal pull between law and lawlessness. That dream is where we begin.

When you sit down to write a Western drama, you're not just writing about a time or a place. You're reaching for something timeless. You're reaching for the soul of the frontier—the fierce independence, the aching loneliness, the unyielding grit of people who lived beyond the edge of civilization. This is a genre that is soaked in struggle, where every man and woman carves out their own fate with bullets, bruises, and broken promises. And the best way to enter that world is to close your eyes, breathe in the dry wind of the plains, and dream.

Western storytelling is built on contrasts. It thrives on tension between chaos and order, between the old world and the new, between native land and settler expansion, between honor and greed. Whether you're writing a novel, a short story, or a screenplay, you need to immerse yourself in this contradiction. The Western world is wild but oddly principled. It's where heroes are haunted and villains are sometimes justified. And it's in this moral gray area that your story takes shape.

Using ChatGPT to explore these themes can be like having a digital co-writer who's always ready with an idea, a plot twist, or even a piece of authentic dialogue. But before you start prompting, you've got to build the emotional world your story lives in. Start with a feeling. Maybe it's loneliness. Maybe it's vengeance. Maybe it's a sense of justice that won't die. These feelings are what drive the great Westerns, from *Unforgiven* to *True Grit* to *Django Unchained*. Feed that emotion into ChatGPT and let it start painting the world around your characters.

Let's say you want to write about a bounty hunter. You don't start by saying "A bounty hunter walks into a town." You start by imagining what kind of man or woman this is. Why do they chase people for money? What drives them to live on the outskirts of the law? What have they lost—or who have they lost—that's made them this way? When you dream of the frontier, you're dreaming of characters born from hardship, shaped by the land, and defined by the choices they make when no one is watching. Those are the kinds of stories readers remember.

It also helps to think visually. Westerns are cinematic by nature. Picture it in your head. A man on horseback, riding across a burnt-orange desert. A saloon door swinging open. A revolver slowly drawn from a worn leather holster. These aren't just visuals; they're promises to the reader. They say, "This story will take you somewhere rugged and real." When working with ChatGPT, use this imagery in your prompts. You'll be amazed at how quickly you can build a scene, a mood, or even a world that feels grounded and authentic.

But dreaming of the frontier isn't just about the obvious visuals. It's about tapping into the deeper mythology of the American West. This includes the struggle between Native American tribes and expanding settlers, the aftermath of the Civil War, the loneliness of the homesteader, and the lure of gold buried deep in the hills. These aren't just plot points. They're part of the emotional and historical gravity that holds your story together. And you can use ChatGPT to explore any of these themes by asking questions and following where the answers lead.

Start with a question: "What was it like to live alone on the frontier after the death of a loved one?" Or "How would a half-Apache gunfighter be received in a post-Civil War town in Texas?" These are the kinds of prompts that give depth and heart to your story. ChatGPT can help you sketch out responses, develop character motivations, and brainstorm conflicts. You're not just dreaming anymore—you're building.

And once you've dreamed it, you can shape it. Dreaming of the frontier is a raw and poetic process. Writing the story is where you turn poetry into structure. But you don't have to do it alone. ChatGPT isn't just a tool for typing—it's a companion for exploration. You can use it to simulate character conversations, write first drafts of scenes, or generate ideas you hadn't thought of yet. It's like throwing your story into the wind and seeing what comes back.

But you, the writer, are still the one in the saddle. You choose the direction. You control the tone, the pace, the morality, and the outcome. You're the one dreaming of the frontier, but you're also the one deciding what the dream means. Does your story end in bloodshed or forgiveness? Does your hero ride off into the sunset or fall to his knees in the dirt? That's up to you. ChatGPT can help you see the paths, but it's your hand that chooses which trail to follow.

The beauty of writing a Western drama is that you're tapping into something bigger than yourself. You're taking a piece of history, a piece of myth, and a piece of your own soul, and fusing them into a story that can ride hard and fast across the imagination. It begins with a dream. A dream of dust, and blood, and wide-open skies. A dream of a place where justice is personal, where every man carries his past on his back, and where every woman has a secret worth dying for. It begins with dreaming of the frontier.

And once you've dreamed it, you'll never stop wanting to write it.

The Power of the Ending: Why We Start at the Finish

When it comes to writing a powerful Western drama, there's something magical about knowing how it ends before you even write the first word. It might seem backwards, but that's the trick. Great storytelling—especially in the Western tradition—comes from understanding where your characters are heading. You're not just spinning a tale into the wind. You're riding hard toward a final moment that will define everything that came before it. That ending is your compass, your guiding star, and it's why we start at the finish.

Think about your favorite Westerns for a moment. There's always that unforgettable final scene. Maybe it's a man bleeding out in the dirt, his final words whispering forgiveness. Maybe it's a woman watching the one man she ever loved ride away forever. Maybe it's a dusty graveyard, a gun still smoking, justice finally served. Whatever it is, it's never just a conclusion. It's a culmination. That ending doesn't just wrap up the story—it gives everything that came before it meaning.

When you sit down with ChatGPT to write your Western, try beginning with that last scene. Literally describe it. Visualize it. Feed it into the model. Tell ChatGPT, "The story ends with a retired gunslinger being buried on Boot Hill by the sheriff he once tried to kill." From that one sentence, you've instantly got the bones of a story. You know the relationship between those two characters is complicated. You know there's a past full of betrayal or redemption. You know the journey will be full of tension. Suddenly, you're not writing blind. You're writing toward something.

Starting with the end gives your story purpose. In a genre like Western drama, where life is rough and choices matter, purpose is everything. If the ending is a showdown in a ghost town at high noon, then every scene before it should build toward that inevitable confrontation. It means every conversation, every decision, every turn of the trail pushes your characters closer to that moment. Without knowing the ending, you risk meandering through the desert. With it, you're charging full speed toward a destination with your guns drawn.

This also helps you control the emotional tone of your story. If you know your story ends in tragedy, then you can use contrast to make it hurt more. Maybe your hero starts off full of hope, thinking he can escape the life of violence. Or maybe he believes in the law, only to see it fail him when it matters most. On the flip side, if your ending is triumphant—say, a long-lost daughter finds her way home to her father—you can choose to make the road there gritty, cruel, and full of false hope. The ending gives your emotions structure.

There's another advantage too. Westerns thrive on myth, and myth is circular. Often, Western stories end where they began, only everything's changed. A man returns to the town he once fled. A woman stands at the same door, waiting for someone who never comes. These are images soaked in poetry, and they carry weight because of what they reflect. If you plan your ending first, you can plant seeds early in your story that will bloom just in time for the final scene. That kind of symmetry doesn't happen by accident—it happens when you start at the finish.

You can also use ChatGPT to test multiple endings before you ever commit to one. Ask it, "What are three different emotional endings for a Western story about a grieving ex-soldier?" You'll likely get a revenge ending, a forgiveness arc, and a self-sacrificial one. Each one will shape your story in a completely different direction. This is how you play with structure without wasting time. You're building a map of possible routes before saddling up.

Let's say your Western ends with the hero throwing down his gun, walking away from a fight. That tells you everything about who this character is—or at least who he's become. So how did he get there? That's your story. Maybe he was once the deadliest gun in the territory, and over the course of the plot, he's haunted by the lives he's taken. The journey is one of reflection and redemption, but the ending was always waiting there for him like a shadow. You don't discover it by accident. You point your story straight at it.

This technique also helps when you're feeling stuck halfway through. All you have to do is look up and ask yourself, "Does this scene move us closer to the ending?" If the answer is no, it doesn't belong. If the answer is yes, it stays. That's how you stay lean and focused, especially when you're trying to write fast or under pressure. With a clear ending in mind, every part of your narrative becomes a stepping stone across the river. You know which direction you're going, and you won't get swept away.

Another benefit is with pacing. Western dramas have a natural rhythm—a build-up, a lull, a storm, and then a hard stop. When you know the ending, you can time these beats like a drum. You'll know when to slow down and let the land speak, and when to turn up the heat with a fast-paced gunfight or confrontation. That's something ChatGPT can help you model. Ask it, "Give me a beat-by-beat structure for a story that ends with a hero's death by betrayal." You'll get a dramatic outline that keeps the tension rising toward your chosen finale.

And finally, the ending lets you say something. Westerns are never just about what happens. They're about what it means. They're morality tales with blood on their hands. So, when you know how your story ends, you can decide what truth you want it to tell. Does justice win, or is it an illusion? Does love survive, or is it lost in the dust? Does the hero ride off into the sunset, or does he disappear into legend? The choice is yours, and it all begins with the end.

So before you write the beginning of your Western drama, take a moment to dream up the final frame. What's the last image the reader sees? What's the final line they hear echo in their mind? Once you know that, you've got everything you need. The trail is clear. The story is waiting. You're just riding it home.

Using ChatGPT to Build Your Western from Scratch

When you set out to write a Western drama, you might be staring at a blank page, wondering where to begin. The beauty of working with ChatGPT is that you never have to start alone. You've got a digital partner ready to throw ideas into the wind and help you build a story from the dust up. But to make the most of this tool, you need to know how to talk to it. You don't ask for a story—you guide one into existence, like a campfire tale being spun under the stars.

Let's say you have no plot, no characters, no setting—nothing but the desire to write something gritty and unforgettable. That's enough. Open up ChatGPT and type something simple, like: *"Help me come up with a Western drama about revenge."* What comes back might be rough, or it might hit you right in the gut. The key is to treat the response not as a script, but as a jumping-off point. Ask follow-up questions. Get curious. Push deeper. That's how you shape raw output into a personal, powerful story.

You might be surprised how fast things develop. One prompt might give you a Civil War veteran tracking down the outlaw who burned his farm. Another could hand you a saloon owner who uncovers the secret past of a newly arrived stranger. Use those sparks to light your fire. You're not locked into any idea. You're just letting ChatGPT help you explore the landscape of possibility, from the dusty border towns to the mountains thick with pine and promise.

Start by defining your main character. Ask ChatGPT: *"Who is my Western protagonist, and what's haunting them?"* That haunting—that wound—is the heart of your drama. Western heroes are rarely clean-cut good guys. They're bruised, broken, running from their past or searching for redemption. ChatGPT can generate layered character profiles with rich emotional depth, and you can adjust them as you go. Maybe you like the idea of a female bounty hunter whose family was murdered when she was a child. That's a whole series of episodes or chapters waiting to be written.

Once you've got a character, ask about setting. Type: *"Describe a unique Western town with secrets and tension."* What you get might be a mining town with a hidden graveyard beneath the church, or a wind-swept trading post ruled by a corrupt marshal. Use those details to sketch your world. Don't settle for generic saloons and dusty roads. Ask for unusual landmarks, local legends, rivalries between townspeople. Let ChatGPT fill your canvas with color. The more specific you get in your prompts, the more vivid your world becomes.

Now it's time to build the structure. You can ask: *"Give me a three-act Western plot with a tragic ending."* ChatGPT might respond with a summary, which you can then expand scene by scene. You can even ask it to break down each act into beats, with emotional turns and key moments. It can map out character arcs, show how relationships develop, and even recommend where to insert action scenes, moments of quiet reflection, and brutal moral choices. If something feels too cliché, just tell it to twist the trope. The AI listens.

For dialogue, you can try: *"Write a tense conversation between a sheriff and the outlaw he once called a friend."* You'll be amazed how quickly voices take shape. If the tone isn't quite right, you can ask it to rewrite it with more grit, more emotion, or more subtlety. You can even give it a line of your own and ask it to continue the exchange. It's like throwing a stone into a canyon and hearing the echo answer back with ideas you hadn't expected.

The real trick is collaboration. Don't expect perfection in one go. Think of ChatGPT as a rough sculptor, giving you the raw shape you'll refine. Keep guiding it. If it gives you a weak motivation for your villain, ask for stronger ones. If your story feels flat, ask how to raise the stakes. The more questions you ask, the more the model learns what kind of story you're trying to tell. And if you ever hit a wall, just change direction. Ask ChatGPT: *"Give me a twist that changes everything."* It might drop a bombshell you never saw coming.

You can also build your story out of images. Ask for visual prompts like: *"Describe a haunting Western landscape at dusk"* or *"Give me the interior of an abandoned church turned hideout."* These descriptions can form the basis of entire scenes. If you're writing a screenplay, ChatGPT can even help format it or create a scene-by-scene outline based on your idea. If you're writing a novel, it can flesh out paragraphs, expand character backstories, and fill in the quiet spaces between the gunshots and galloping horses.

Western drama thrives on emotional contrast. Peace and violence. Love and vengeance. Law and chaos. ChatGPT can help you explore those contrasts through theme development. Try: *"What are some emotional themes for a Western story about a man returning home after war?"* You might get loneliness, guilt, betrayal, hope. Pick one or two and build your scenes around them. Your story becomes more than a shootout or a ride through the desert—it becomes a meditation on survival and identity.

Even pacing becomes easier with ChatGPT. Ask: *"How should I pace a Western novel so the tension keeps building?"* You'll get a breakdown of rising action, key reversals, and climax timing. Want something faster? Ask how to turn it into a short story. Want to stretch it into a serialized drama? Ask for episode ideas. You're not limited by format—you're empowered by it. That's the beauty of building your Western from scratch with this kind of creative partner.

But remember this—ChatGPT is a guide, not the author. You are the voice. The emotion. The will. Use the tool to find new trails, but it's your hand that writes the story. Don't be afraid to go off the suggested path. Sometimes the best Westerns aren't the ones that follow tradition—they're the ones that reshape it. You might start with a revenge story and end with forgiveness. You might think your hero is a man of the law and discover he's been the outlaw all along.

So when you sit down to build your Western from scratch, don't worry about what you don't know. Worry about what you feel. Plug your instincts into ChatGPT and see what blooms. Write like you're chasing a storm. Edit like you're sharpening a blade. And remember, the frontier is wide open. You don't need to walk it alone. You've got a story to tell—and a partner to help you ride it home.

Cowboys and Outlaws: Creating Legendary Archetypes

One of the most exciting parts of writing a Western drama is breathing life into the archetypes that define the genre. Cowboys and outlaws are more than just hats, spurs, and six-shooters—they're symbols. They're walking contradictions. They carry the weight of freedom and rebellion, law and lawlessness, survival and sacrifice. These characters don't just populate your story—they *are* the story. And with ChatGPT as your co-writer, you can go deeper than the stereotypes and create legends in every scene.

To begin with, let's talk about the cowboy. He's not just a cattle herder. He's often a loner, a drifter, a man with a past he doesn't talk about and a future he's not chasing. He may ride for a brand, but he rides harder for his own sense of right and wrong. The cowboy is often the moral center of a Western, but that doesn't mean he's always clean. His hands are usually dirty with regret, blood, or the dust of a thousand miles. When you create a cowboy character, you're not writing a hero—you're writing a myth wrapped in muscle and silence.

Ask ChatGPT to help you build your cowboy. Try something like: *"Describe a cowboy who once led a gang but now rides alone, haunted by his past."* You'll get a detailed character sketch, probably with a tragic backstory, scars, and some deep moral conflict. You can follow that up with: *"What would this cowboy do if he came across a gang raiding a peaceful town?"* From there, a story starts to form. You're not just building a character—you're building their legend.

Now the outlaw—he's just as vital, and sometimes more interesting. An outlaw isn't always evil. In fact, some of the best outlaws are former heroes. The line between outlaw and cowboy is razor-thin. One follows the law; the other spits on it. But they might both believe in justice. What separates them is often how far they're willing to go to get it. Some outlaws are sadistic, sure, but others are Robin Hood figures, stealing from corrupt banks, exacting revenge on crooked sheriffs, or fighting against land barons who stole everything from their families.

To shape your outlaw, feed ChatGPT a scenario: *"Give me an outlaw character who was betrayed by his best friend, now the town's sheriff."* Right away, you've got a character with grit, pain, and motive. Then go further: *"What does he believe in, and what won't he do?"* You'll uncover a moral code, which is often more compelling than law itself. A well-crafted outlaw is dangerous not because he's lawless, but because he's principled in his own twisted way. That principle gives him strength, purpose, and narrative power.

What's exciting is that these two archetypes—the cowboy and the outlaw—often reflect each other. They can start off as enemies and end as allies, or vice versa. One might see a part of himself in the other. That mirroring creates tension, especially when they're on opposite sides of a conflict. Think of a cowboy hired to bring in an outlaw who saved his life years ago. Or an outlaw forced to protect a town because the only woman he ever loved is in it. These are the kinds of complex dynamics that turn a simple shootout into a gripping, unforgettable drama.

ChatGPT can help you map these relationships quickly. Try: *"Describe the emotional bond between a cowboy and an outlaw who grew up together but took different paths."* This prompt will produce character history, motivations, and dramatic stakes that practically write the story for you. Then you can use follow-ups to dig deeper: *"What secret are they both hiding?"* or *"What event tore them apart?"* These kinds of layers take your story from flat to epic.

You can also reverse expectations. Who says the cowboy has to be a man? Why can't the most feared outlaw be an aging woman with a bounty on her head and no fear in her heart? ChatGPT doesn't have biases unless you write them in. You can build a band of cowboys that includes former slaves, immigrants, young orphans, or Indigenous fighters. Every character can reflect a different thread of the American frontier experience. The key is to let the archetype guide the form, but let your creativity shape the soul.

And don't forget the dynamic between these archetypes and the world around them. The cowboy often represents a fading way of life—a man caught between the wilderness and civilization. The outlaw may represent rebellion against an unjust system or the violent cost of unchecked freedom. These themes give your story weight. Ask ChatGPT: *"What societal changes threatened the cowboy way of life in the 1880s?"* or *"Why might a man become an outlaw in post-Civil War Texas?"* These historical details aren't just window dressing—they breathe truth into your fiction.

When you write a Western drama, you're not just creating characters—you're crafting legends that walk, speak, and bleed across the land. The cowboy and the outlaw are two sides of the same coin, spinning through every campfire tale and gunpowder-laced showdown you write. With ChatGPT, you can sculpt these figures from scratch, break them down, rebuild them, and let them ride across a world of your own making.

The most iconic stories begin with a cowboy's silence and end with an outlaw's last stand. And in between, there's everything you want to explore—loss, redemption, betrayal, love, vengeance, loyalty, and the longing to belong in a world that's always changing. Let ChatGPT help you shape that journey. Let your characters become the kind that readers don't forget. Because in the West, the line between good and bad isn't drawn in the dirt. It's carved into the heart.

The Gunfighter's Mind: Understanding the Lone Killer

The Western gunfighter is one of the most iconic figures in all of storytelling. He's the shadow in the corner of the saloon, the man who speaks with his eyes and kills with precision. He walks alone, often not because he wants to—but because the world no longer fits him, or he no longer fits the world. To write a compelling Western drama, you've got to understand the mind of the gunfighter. Not the caricature, not the surface-level bravado—but the psychology of the lone killer. This is a man whose silence speaks volumes, whose every step echoes with purpose, and whose soul has seen too much.

When you use ChatGPT to help create this kind of character, it helps to begin with a question that strikes at the heart of his solitude. Ask: *"Why does this gunfighter live alone, far from town?"* The response might touch on betrayal, grief, war, or even a philosophical detachment from society. Whatever answer you get, you can start building a profile of a man who isn't just dangerous—he's dangerous for a reason. This is someone who has made peace with violence, or maybe never has, and carries that tension in every breath.

The gunfighter is often a man at war with himself. Maybe he killed his first man too young, and that moment defined everything that came after. Maybe he's spent years on the run from a past that still lives in his dreams. Maybe he only draws when he must, but when he does, there's no hesitation. He's developed a sixth sense for danger, a radar for dishonesty, and a code of ethics that might seem twisted to the outside world—but to him, it's the only compass that matters. Ask ChatGPT: *"What is the personal code of a gunfighter who refuses to shoot a man in the back, no matter the cost?"* and see how quickly the story starts to bloom.

You can use ChatGPT to simulate internal monologues too. Try: *"Write the thoughts of a gunfighter waiting for a duel at dawn."* The reply might be haunted and poetic, a mixture of calculation, memory, and cold resolve. This is the texture you want for your character. The duel itself is just the tip of the iceberg. The real drama lies in what's happening inside his head before the first draw. What's at stake? What does he stand to lose or gain? Has he done this a hundred times before, or is this the one fight that truly matters?

Gunfighters in Western dramas are rarely just killers. They're thinkers. Strategists. Men of few words but sharp minds. They calculate risk constantly, read people with a glance, and always know where the exits are. In this way, the gunfighter resembles a philosopher as much as a warrior. Ask ChatGPT: *"What kind of childhood might create a man who survives only by the gun?"* You'll find yourself peeling back the layers to discover a boy who was abandoned, abused, orphaned, or thrown into violence too early. That backstory won't just inform your plot—it will shape every word of dialogue and every choice the character makes.

Sometimes the gunfighter doesn't want to kill anymore. That's where the real tension lives. He's fast—maybe the fastest—but each kill is a reminder of the man he used to be. Maybe he drinks to forget. Maybe he refuses to carry more than six bullets. Maybe he's looking for peace, even though peace never seems to be looking for him. With ChatGPT, you can build out those habits and quirks. Prompt it with: *"What are the daily rituals of a gunfighter trying to avoid a fight?"* and see how that plays into your story. Maybe he sharpens his knife not because he wants to use it, but because it keeps his hands busy. Maybe he doesn't sleep in beds—just near exits.

And what about regret? Gunfighters are often surrounded by ghosts. Some they've buried. Others they left behind. Ask ChatGPT to explore that: *"Who does this gunfighter dream about at night, and why?"* Let the answer surprise you. Maybe it's a brother he betrayed. A lover who tried to change him. A child he never got to raise. These ghosts are what make the gunfighter more than a killer. They make him human. And it's that fragile humanity that your audience will cling to, even when the bullets fly.

Another layer of the gunfighter's psychology is his relationship with death. It's not just something he causes—it's something he lives beside. He's seen friends die, watched enemies fall, and maybe he's even been shot and left for dead. He walks with death like an old friend. He doesn't fear it, but he respects it. That gives him a calm most men don't have. You can use ChatGPT to explore this mindset. Ask: *"What does death mean to a man who has faced it a hundred times?"* and let that reflection infuse your character's voice and actions.

You can also dig into how the world sees him. Is he a legend or a ghost? Is his name whispered in fear, or has it faded into myth? Maybe townsfolk warn their children about him. Maybe other gunfighters seek him out to make their own names. That reputation can become both armor and curse. Prompt ChatGPT with: *"What do people say about a gunfighter who hasn't drawn in ten years?"* and let the rumors shape your story. You might find out that the silence is louder than any gunshot.

But don't forget—your gunfighter doesn't exist in a vacuum. He lives in a world filled with lawmen, thieves, bartenders, widows, bounty hunters, and people just trying to get by. How he interacts with them matters. Maybe he respects the sheriff, but refuses to work with him. Maybe he saves a boy from a street brawl, then vanishes without a word. Every encounter adds to the mystery. Ask ChatGPT to simulate those scenes: *"Describe the interaction between a gunfighter and a widow who runs the general store."* You might find unexpected softness, friction, or regret—and that's where your story deepens.

Ultimately, the gunfighter is a man burdened by survival. He's not flashy. He's not theatrical. He's deliberate, efficient, and alone. But within that solitude is a depth of emotion just waiting to be explored. With ChatGPT, you can bring those layers to the surface, crafting a character who feels like he stepped right off the frontier and into your imagination.

So don't just write a man with a fast draw. Write a man with a heavy heart. Write a man whose mind is as dangerous as his aim. Let your audience fear him, admire him, and mourn him—sometimes all at once. That's how you understand the gunfighter. That's how you create the kind of character who leaves bullet holes not just in the saloon wall, but in the reader's soul.

Lawmen and Desperados: Crafting Conflict with a Badge

One of the richest veins to tap in Western drama is the ongoing war between those who uphold the law and those who spit in its face. The lawman and the desperado are two opposing forces constantly circling one another, often cut from the same cloth. Sometimes, they're even the same man, just split by time or circumstance. When you write Westerns using ChatGPT, this dynamic can give your story a dramatic core that crackles with tension. The badge means something in the West—but it doesn't always mean justice.

To get started, think about the role of the lawman. He isn't just a sheriff with a star on his chest. He's often the only thing standing between order and chaos in a town on the edge of the world. But that doesn't mean he's clean. Many Western lawmen were just the toughest men willing to take the job. They're often former outlaws themselves, or veterans who traded one kind of violence for another. When you sit down with ChatGPT, start by asking: *"Describe a sheriff who used to be a bank robber."* You'll immediately have a character with tension built into his bones. He wears the badge, but does he still carry the outlaw's instincts?

Now consider the desperado. He's not just a killer—he's a force of disruption. He challenges the boundaries of what society allows. He might be a cold-blooded villain, but he might also be a man pushed too far by an unfair world. Ask ChatGPT: *"Give me a desperado who turned to crime after the railroad stole his family's land."* Now you've got someone with a cause, not just a gun. The best antagonists in Western drama are the ones who believe they're doing the right thing, or at least doing the only thing left to them. That belief gives them power.

Once you've got your lawman and your desperado, it's time to explore the space between them. Maybe they were once friends. Maybe one mentored the other before they took different paths. Maybe they're brothers, separated by ideology. You can ask ChatGPT: *"Describe the relationship between a marshal and a wanted man who used to ride together."* The results can fuel your entire plot, because that personal history creates emotional stakes. When a lawman has to bring in someone he once trusted, the line between duty and conscience gets blurred—and that's where great Western drama lives.

Conflict in this dynamic doesn't always have to be physical. The best scenes are the ones where two men sit across from each other, words like bullets. A sheriff warning a gang leader to leave town by sundown. A bandit daring the marshal to shoot first. These are moments soaked in silence, tension, and unresolved emotion. You can use ChatGPT to simulate these dialogues. Ask: *"Write a tense conversation between a sheriff and the outlaw who killed his deputy."* Then tweak the tone—make it colder, more regretful, or more venomous—until it feels right for your story.

You can also let the conflict play out in the town itself. Maybe the lawman is trying to clean up a town run by the desperado's gang. Maybe the outlaw has friends in high places, and the sheriff has none. Maybe the townsfolk are scared to choose sides. Ask ChatGPT to describe the social atmosphere of a town under outlaw control. Then ask what tactics the sheriff might use to take it back. You'll get ideas for scenes, character interactions, and the kind of slow-burn tension that can carry an entire episode or chapter.

The badge doesn't always protect a man. Sometimes, it makes him a target. Especially in a place where justice is negotiable and survival is a daily battle. Maybe your lawman starts to question whether he's doing the right thing. Maybe he starts bending the rules. Maybe he becomes more like the man he's hunting. Ask ChatGPT: *"What would drive a lawman to break the law in order to protect his town?"* The answers might surprise you—and they might change your story for the better.

On the flip side, maybe your desperado wants out. Maybe he's tired of running, tired of killing, and just wants one last chance at peace. That kind of internal conflict can make for an unforgettable redemption arc. But it doesn't come easy in the West. The past always rides close behind. Use ChatGPT to explore his struggle: *"Describe a scene where an outlaw tries to surrender but the sheriff won't forgive him."* That one moment can hold all the weight of a gunfight without a single shot being fired.

The relationship between lawmen and desperados isn't just good versus evil. It's two men trying to define what justice means in a lawless world. One enforces order, the other disrupts it—but both are responding to the same broken system. That's the depth you want to tap into. With ChatGPT, you can play out every scenario—what if the lawman is corrupt and the outlaw is noble? What if they're both wrong? What if the only law is survival? These questions turn your story from a Western into a drama that just happens to be set in the West.

Even side characters can enrich the conflict. Maybe the deputy sympathizes with the outlaws. Maybe the outlaw's daughter is in love with the sheriff. Maybe a preacher is trying to broker peace between the two. Use ChatGPT to brainstorm character webs. Ask: *"Who else in town is caught in the conflict between the lawman and the outlaw?"* Suddenly, your story gains weight, complexity, and a sense of inevitability.

At the end of the day, the badge is just a piece of metal. What matters is the man who wears it—and the man who challenges it. The lawman and the desperado will always find each other, in dusty streets and dark corners, because they're bound by fate, history, and something deeper: the need to prove which way of life is worth dying for. Let ChatGPT help you build that showdown. Let it guide the bullets, the silences, and the choices that shape legends. Because in the world of Western drama, conflict with a badge is never just about law—it's about legacy.

The Bounty Hunter's Code: Writing for Gold and Justice

If there's one character in Western drama who walks the line between outlaw and lawman with spurs clicking and eyes sharp, it's the bounty hunter. This is a figure who lives outside the system but works within it just enough to keep his head above water. He doesn't wear a badge, but he carries a sense of justice—his own brand of it. He'll bring in a killer for a sack of gold, but he might just as easily turn on the man who hired him if the deal smells rotten. When writing a bounty hunter, you're not just crafting a character—you're crafting a philosophy. And every line he speaks, every choice he makes, comes back to that personal code.

Start by understanding the world he moves through. The bounty hunter isn't tied to one town. He rides alone, across territories, chasing whispers and rumors, surviving on instinct and skill. People don't welcome him, and they don't mourn him when he leaves. He's often the last face a fugitive sees and the last hope a grieving family clings to. That in-between space—where law doesn't quite reach and chaos thrives—is where your bounty hunter shines. And that's where your story can dig its spurs in deep.

Using ChatGPT, you can develop this kind of character from the ground up. Try a prompt like: *"Describe a bounty hunter who only brings in fugitives alive—never dead."* That simple rule becomes the seed for an entire character arc. Why doesn't he kill? Maybe he once did and can't stomach it anymore. Maybe he believes that only the law has the right to pass final judgment. Or maybe it's because he's seen too much blood already, and he's trying to hold on to some sliver of decency. Whatever the reason, it becomes his code. It becomes the thing that separates him from the outlaws he hunts—and from the lawmen who sometimes shoot first and ask later.

Then ask: *"What would force this bounty hunter to break his own rule?"* Now you've got conflict. Now you've got a story. You're exploring not just the chase, but the personal stakes behind every decision. And that's where a great Western drama really begins to take form—not with the gun, but with the man holding it.

The bounty hunter's code is what makes him compelling. Maybe he refuses to work for a corrupt sheriff. Maybe he only takes bounties on men who hurt women and children. Maybe he gives half his reward money to widows, or maybe he never works for gold at all—just closure. The more specific you get with that code, the more grounded and unique your character becomes. Ask ChatGPT to help you list personal rules, then pick two or three that define your bounty hunter's world. You're not writing a hired gun. You're writing a man who's chosen to live by a set of principles—principles he'll fight for, even if no one else understands them.

And don't forget the practical side of the job. The life of a bounty hunter is dirty, dangerous, and full of uncertainty. He sleeps in the wild. He faces ambushes. He tracks men who are as desperate as they are deadly. Ask ChatGPT to describe the daily routine of a bounty hunter tracking a fugitive through a mountain pass. You'll get ideas for the physical world of your story—snow in the boots, gunpowder in the nostrils, the echo of hoof-beats on stone. These details bring your drama to life and show the toll the work takes on a man.

You can also dive into the emotional burden. The bounty hunter may try to stay detached, but he's human. Maybe he sees himself in the men he tracks down. Maybe he's haunted by a bounty he didn't bring back alive. Maybe every reward poster is a mirror he's forced to look into. Try asking ChatGPT: *"What memories keep a bounty hunter awake at night?"* The responses will open doors to flashbacks, regrets, and the kind of inner struggle that makes readers care even when your character doesn't say much.

The chase is central to Western storytelling, and nobody chases better than a bounty hunter. But the chase isn't just about distance—it's about purpose. Maybe your bounty hunter is chasing someone who knows the truth about his past. Maybe he's hunting a man who once saved his life, or a woman who disappeared years ago and has resurfaced with a bounty on her head. These complications add layers to the story. Ask ChatGPT for scenarios like: *"Create a bounty hunter plot where the target is a former lover."* That's not just a job—it's a storm waiting to happen.

Your bounty hunter can also serve as a reflection of the world around him. In a corrupt town, he becomes a reluctant enforcer of justice. In a lawless stretch of wilderness, he becomes a judge. In a world where no one can be trusted, his personal code becomes more valuable than gold. Through him, your story can explore what justice really means. Ask ChatGPT: *"How would a bounty hunter react to bringing in a man he believes is innocent?"* That's not just a twist—it's a moral crucible, and it makes for unforgettable storytelling.

And don't forget how others see him. Townsfolk might fear him. Outlaws might respect him. Sheriffs might resent him. Preachers might try to save him. The bounty hunter walks into every scene with a weight. He's not part of the town, but he changes it just by being there. Ask ChatGPT: *"How would a frontier town react to the arrival of a legendary bounty hunter?"* The response can give you social tension, subplots, and even new characters. Maybe a boy idolizes him. Maybe a mother spits at his boots. These reactions say just as much about him as his own words.

In the end, the bounty hunter is a man pulled in opposite directions—between justice and survival, between gold and guilt, between the man he was and the man he's trying to become. Writing him means walking that same line. With ChatGPT, you can explore every angle of his mind, his motives, and his memories. Let the AI help you build his world, test his resolve, and throw obstacles in his path.

And remember: the bounty hunter doesn't wear a badge, but he's still got a code. And that code, once broken, might be the last thing holding him together. Writing for gold and justice isn't about finding balance—it's about watching what happens when those two things clash. That's where drama lives. That's where legends are made.

The American Civil War as Western Backdrop

If you really want to inject your Western drama with weight, history, and emotional complexity, look no further than the American Civil War. This wasn't just a war fought in the East over blue and gray uniforms—it was a seismic event that rippled through every dusty trail, outlaw camp, and frontier town across the West. The war shaped the minds of the men who survived it, broke the families it touched, and transformed the lawless territories into uneasy places of redefinition. When you set your Western against the backdrop of the Civil War or its aftermath, you're tapping into a well of conflict that doesn't need much to boil over.

ChatGPT can help you build this atmosphere piece by piece. Ask something like: *"Describe a former Confederate soldier arriving in a New Mexico town in 1870."* From that prompt, you'll get not only a visual setting but an emotional one. You'll get a man shaped by defeat, still carrying the ideology or scars of war, walking into a place that might be populated by Union sympathizers, freed slaves, displaced Native tribes, and immigrants trying to forget the war even happened. That kind of layered tension makes for strong drama.

The Civil War isn't just backstory in a Western—it's a force that continues to pull at your characters long after the guns have gone silent. Many iconic Western archetypes can trace their edges back to the war. The drifter may be a soldier who couldn't go home. The outlaw might be someone who learned how to kill under a flag and never figured out how to stop. The lawman could be a former Union cavalry officer trying to bring some sense of order to a world he once helped destroy. Each of these paths leads to characters that feel real, raw, and wounded.

Ask ChatGPT to help you write these internal wounds. Something like: *"What kind of nightmares might haunt a Civil War veteran turned bounty hunter?"* You'll be flooded with ideas—smoke-choked battlefields, friends dying with their eyes open, orders that led to massacres, regrets carved deep into memory. That trauma becomes part of the fabric of your character. He's not just a gunman—he's a survivor. That adds depth to every choice he makes, even when he's silent.

And the war wasn't over just because the armies disbanded. In the West, it lingered like smoke. Ask ChatGPT to describe a town divided by old loyalties. You might get a saloon where ex-Union and ex-Confederate soldiers avoid eye contact, a church split by ideology, a local government still choosing sides. These aren't just background details. They're conflict, ready to ignite. Maybe your protagonist walks into this powder keg and accidentally lights the fuse. Or maybe he's the fuse.

You can also use the war to shape motivations. Ask: *"Why would a Union deserter become an outlaw after the war?"* The answers might be economic, moral, or deeply personal. He saw too much blood, followed too many lies, and now doesn't believe in anything. Or maybe he's trying to raise money to bring his family out West and sees no other way. Those shades of gray are what make Westerns great. You don't want clean-cut heroes and moustache-twirling villains. You want men and women shaped by impossible choices—and the Civil War was a furnace of those choices.

One of the most compelling elements of using the Civil War in your story is how it can twist the idea of justice. The West is already a lawless place, but add in former soldiers who believe their side was right—and still do—and you've got a real mess on your hands. A man might hang another for being a "traitor," even though the war's been over for five years. An ex-Confederate sheriff might refuse to protect a Black family settling on the edge of town. Ask ChatGPT to write a confrontation between a freed slave and a former Confederate officer in a Western town. The emotional weight will hit like a hammer. And from that moment, a story can unfold.

Don't forget the opportunities for visual storytelling either. A tattered Union coat worn beneath a duster. A battlefield turned ghost town. A rusted saber hanging above the bar in a saloon. These are relics that don't just say "this happened"—they say "this is still happening, in the minds of the people who lived it." You can ask ChatGPT: *"What kinds of physical reminders of the Civil War might appear in a Western town in 1875?"* and you'll get a catalog of mood-setting, symbol-rich details that can help paint every scene with authenticity.

The war also gives you access to powerful themes—loyalty, betrayal, loss, redemption, trauma, division, and the desperate need to rebuild. Whether your character is trying to forget the war or still fighting it in his heart, that struggle can form the emotional spine of your story. ChatGPT can help you tie these themes directly into character arcs. Ask: *"How can a former soldier find peace in a land that still feels like a battlefield?"* That question alone can write a whole novel.

You can also explore regional perspectives. The Western territories were not neatly aligned with North or South. Many people were simply trying to survive. Some towns may have never chosen a side. Others may have changed sides mid-war. Ask ChatGPT to describe the political atmosphere of Arizona or Kansas during and after the war, and you'll be able to weave in historical tensions that make your world feel fully alive.

The American Civil War may have ended in 1865, but in a Western drama, it never really ends. It's a shadow, a scar, and sometimes, a ghost. It lives in every man who walks the trail with blood on his conscience and in every town where grudges still burn. By using ChatGPT to explore this backdrop, you're not just giving your story historical weight—you're giving it emotional gravity. You're grounding the myth of the West in a moment of real, lasting upheaval.

So when you write your Western, don't be afraid to let the war walk into your story. Let it sit beside your characters, whisper into their choices, twist their loyalties, and shape the land they ride through. Because a Western drama with the Civil War at its back doesn't just show us the past—it shows us how hard it is to outrun it.

After the Smoke Clears: Post-War Trauma in the West

The war might be over, but for many men and women in the West, it never really ended. After the smoke clears, the real battle begins—the one inside. Post-war trauma isn't just a subplot in Western drama. It's often the entire reason your character is who they are. Whether they fought for the Union or the Confederacy, or whether they lost a brother, a home, or a belief in anything worth fighting for, the wounds of war leave their mark. The West became a place where broken people wandered, trying to find meaning again in the open sky, the saloon bottle, or the barrel of a gun. And that's exactly where your story finds its heartbeat.

Using ChatGPT to write characters with post-war trauma is about more than just listing their flashbacks or mentioning they "don't talk much anymore." It's about understanding how deeply war changes a person, especially when there's no one around to help them unpack what they saw or did. The frontier didn't offer therapy. It offered silence. And for some, that silence screamed louder than any cannon ever could.

Start with a simple prompt like: *"Describe a former Union soldier struggling with guilt in a Western frontier town."* ChatGPT will give you a rough sketch, but the more you refine it, the deeper you'll get. Maybe this soldier was part of a massacre. Maybe he left a friend behind. Maybe he lost faith in the cause he bled for. These kinds of psychological burdens don't just shape character—they shape behavior. He drinks too much. He wakes up screaming. He avoids crowds, flinches at sudden sounds, or starts every day with his back against a wall. Those are the quiet details that tell the story before a single word of dialogue is spoken.

You can also look at how post-war trauma twists relationships. Maybe your character comes back to a town that moved on without him. His girl married someone else. His farm's been sold off. The world kept spinning, but he's stuck somewhere back in the smoke of battle. Ask ChatGPT: *"What would a returning soldier feel if his hometown no longer recognized him?"* and you'll get emotional fuel for chapters of slow-burning internal conflict. This sense of disconnection is a powerful force in Western drama. It pushes characters into solitude, into danger, and sometimes into violence—not because they're evil, but because they've forgotten how to be human in a world that no longer fits.

Trauma in the West often comes out sideways. A former officer becomes a bounty hunter, chasing men because it feels like justice, or maybe penance. A soldier turns outlaw because he can't stop seeing enemies. A man who survived the war now can't let anyone close because too many have died in his arms. Ask ChatGPT: *"How would trauma from the Civil War manifest in a gunslinger's behavior?"* The answers will shape your character's tone, habits, and moral compass. Maybe he won't carry a rifle because the sound reminds him of the battlefield. Maybe he can't kill anymore, or maybe he can't stop.

Post-war trauma doesn't always come from fighting, either. Civilians, freed slaves, widows, and children all carried their own burdens. A woman who nursed soldiers on both sides. A Black man who fought for freedom and now finds none. A child who saw their home burned to the ground. These voices deserve space in your story too. Ask ChatGPT to help build them: *"Describe the emotional journey of a freed slave who settles in a hostile Western town after the war."* You'll get depth that widens your narrative world and gives weight to every choice your protagonist makes.

The environment of the West mirrors trauma in its own way. It's vast, empty, and merciless. Characters with internal scars are drawn to the isolation, hoping to outrun their memories or bury them beneath the silence of the plains. But isolation doesn't heal. It festers. That's why Westerns often end in confrontation—not just with an enemy, but with the self. The land brings it out. You can ask ChatGPT to describe symbolic Western landscapes that reflect emotional trauma—burnt fields, abandoned forts, ghost towns full of echoes. These places become characters in their own right.

Let's not forget how trauma affects storytelling rhythm. Characters who are haunted don't move fast. Their stories are slow burns. Their thoughts linger. Their scenes hang in the air longer than most. This changes how you write your pacing. Ask ChatGPT: *"How can I structure a Western story to reflect a character's PTSD?"* You'll get suggestions for moments of hesitation, repetition, breakdowns, and even the eventual emotional breakthrough. The arc of healing—or at least understanding—isn't rushed. In Western drama, it's hard-earned, and not always complete.

Then there's the element of guilt. Many post-war characters carry survivor's guilt. Why them? Why not the man beside them? That guilt might drive them into danger, make them take jobs no sane man would take, or lead them to protect others at the cost of their own life. You can ask ChatGPT: *"How does survivor's guilt influence a character's choices in a Western narrative?"* and from that, design a path where the character is not just escaping something, but chasing redemption—even if they never say it out loud.

And what about society's reaction to trauma? The West wasn't known for its compassion. If a man talked to himself or had screaming fits in the middle of the night, folks might call him crazy or cursed. This adds another layer of conflict—how your character's suffering is perceived by the community. Does anyone reach out? Does anyone understand? Or is he labeled and pushed further into the wild? Ask ChatGPT: *"How would townsfolk treat a veteran suffering from visible trauma in 1870?"* and use the answer to design social dynamics, friendships, or even romantic tension.

In the Western, trauma becomes a kind of myth. These characters don't wear their wounds on their sleeves. They bury them deep, but those wounds still bleed into every scene, every word, every silence. That's the drama. That's the story. And ChatGPT is here to help you dig into it from every angle. Ask questions, chase memories, follow dreams that turn to nightmares. Use the silence as much as the gunfire. And don't be afraid to let your character break a little. Because in the West, strength isn't about never falling—it's about what you do after you hit the dirt.

So after the smoke clears, don't let the story end. Let it begin. That's when the real journey starts. Not across the plains, but through the wreckage of a soul trying to make peace with a world that kept on spinning while they were stuck in the thunder. That's Western drama. That's where the truth rides in.

Writing a Western with Purpose and Passion

Writing a Western drama isn't about dusting off an old genre and putting hats on characters. It's about reaching deep into your soul and pulling out a story that feels as wide and wild as the frontier itself. It's about telling tales of men and women who don't just ride through landscapes—they are shaped by them. When you write a Western with purpose and passion, you're not copying what's been done. You're adding your voice to a myth that never stopped evolving. You're drawing from the past to say something about the present. That's the power of this genre—and it only works when you care enough to mean every word.

Purpose is what separates a good Western from a great one. It's the *why* behind the gunfights, the chases, the lonely sunsets, and the hardened stares. Maybe you're writing about justice. Maybe about grief. Maybe you want to show how revenge poisons the soul or how forgiveness is harder than any duel. Whatever your message is, it should burn like coal under your story. It doesn't have to be obvious, but it needs to be there, powering the journey from the first word to the last. Ask ChatGPT: *"What are powerful themes for a Western story about loss and redemption?"* You'll get a list of ideas that can give your narrative that needed emotional spine.

Then there's passion. That's what keeps you coming back to the story even when it feels like a dry well. Passion is what turns a generic shootout into a moment of character revelation. It's what gives your characters truth, even if they're fictional. Passion comes through in the small things—a trembling hand before a duel, a long pause before answering a simple question, a sunset that feels like a farewell. You don't write that because you have to. You write it because it *matters*.

With ChatGPT, you can blend purpose and passion into your writing by staying focused on what your story is really *about*. Ask: *"Help me write a Western where a woman returns to the town that betrayed her."* What you'll get is more than a plot—it's a spark. It's the beginning of a story that matters. Then keep pressing: *"Why did they betray her? What does she want? What would it take for her to forgive them?"* You're not just creating scenes. You're sculpting meaning, layer by layer, until your story bleeds truth.

Sometimes, passion comes from a single image. A child standing in a burned field. A bloodied man staring into a cracked mirror. A horse waiting outside a jailhouse as thunder rolls in. These moments don't need dialogue to carry weight. You can feed those visuals into ChatGPT and ask: *"Write a scene based on this image."* Let the AI help you find the words, but bring your heart to the shaping of it. A Western isn't a formula. It's a feeling—gritty, raw, untamed.

Writing with purpose also means being honest about what you're writing. If your story takes place in the post-Civil War West, don't gloss over the realities. Talk about how the war changed people. Talk about how Native Americans were treated. Talk about the pain, the inequality, the resilience, and the survival. Don't write just for entertainment. Write because these stories deserve to be told with weight. If your outlaw is a freed slave turned avenger, write him with truth. Ask ChatGPT for historical context. Ask about the attitudes of the time, the landscape, the politics. Let the facts deepen your fiction.

Passion also means daring to care about your characters more than the plot. It means letting them make decisions that hurt, that surprise, that feel inevitable only in hindsight. You don't need them to be likable—you need them to be *real*. Give them something to fight for. Give them flaws they can't shake and dreams they can't admit. Ask ChatGPT to help define their wounds, their hopes, their regrets. Build a life around them. If you can love or hate your character like a person you've known for years, that's when the story starts to breathe.

And don't forget to write for yourself first. Forget what readers want, what trends say, or what sells. Westerns that endure were never written to check a box. They were written because someone had something to say—about power, or loneliness, or courage, or death. Your job is to find what you care about and put it on the page with no apology. That's where the fire comes from. That's what will move a reader, whether your story ends in blood, redemption, or a long ride into nowhere.

If you're ever stuck, tell ChatGPT: *"Help me rediscover the emotional core of this Western."* It might help you remember why you started the story in the first place. Because you saw something. Felt something. Wanted to say something. Maybe it was about a father and a son. Maybe about a woman who outlived every man who ever tried to own her. Maybe about a man who finally found peace at the end of a rifle. That fire—that voice—that *why* is what gives your story weight.

A Western written without passion is just a series of tropes. A Western written with passion becomes a legend.

So ride into your story with meaning in your heart and dust on your boots. Let every scene serve the message you believe in. Let every character speak from a place of truth, no matter how ugly or beautiful that truth may be. Write like the West depends on it. Because in the end, writing a Western with purpose and passion isn't just about telling a story. It's about making that story *matter*.

Plotting the Chase: Tension, Speed, and Escalation

At the beating heart of every great Western drama lies the chase. It might be a lawman hunting down an outlaw, a bounty hunter tracking a fugitive across harsh terrain, or a desperate soul running from a past that refuses to stay buried. No matter what form it takes, the chase is more than horses and gunfire—it's a test of will, endurance, and morality. It's the engine that drives the story forward and pushes your characters to their limits. And if you want to write a gripping Western, you've got to learn how to plot that chase with tension, speed, and escalation.

The key to a good chase is understanding that it's not just physical—it's emotional. The chase has to mean something to both the pursuer and the pursued. It's not enough that someone's running and someone else is chasing. Ask yourself *why*. What's at stake? What does the chaser need to prove? What does the one being chased stand to lose, or win, if they get away? This emotional fuel gives the chase its fire. You can use ChatGPT to dig deeper. Try: *"Describe the emotional motivation of a bounty hunter chasing a former friend."* What you get back might be the skeleton of a compelling storyline that practically writes itself.

When building your chase, the first thing to consider is speed. But not speed in terms of constant motion—speed in terms of rhythm. A good chase is all about tempo. It should start with a burst—an ambush, a jailbreak, or a sudden betrayal—and then pulse with alternating moments of movement and stillness. A chase that never slows down is exhausting. But one that uses quiet pauses to build dread will hook the reader or viewer and keep them invested. Ask ChatGPT to help you plan pacing: *"Create a beat-by-beat chase sequence with moments of tension and calm."* You'll get a structure you can twist and build upon, from the initial break to the final confrontation.

Escalation is what keeps the chase from going stale. Each beat of the story should raise the stakes. Maybe the terrain gets rougher. Maybe the chaser is wounded. Maybe the pursued gains allies or takes hostages. Every new step should make the situation more dangerous, more personal, or more morally complicated. Ask ChatGPT: *"List ways to escalate a Western chase through a canyon region."* You'll get environmental obstacles, tactical shifts, and psychological turning points that keep the reader leaning forward.

One of the most effective ways to build tension is to let the audience know what the characters don't. Maybe the chaser thinks they're close, but the fugitive has doubled back. Maybe the fugitive is hiding in plain sight, just a heartbeat away from capture. These layers of dramatic irony allow you to stretch tension until it snaps. Try asking ChatGPT: *"Write a scene where a sheriff almost finds the outlaw but just misses him."* Then build variations. Change the timing. Move the setting. Make the sheriff suspect but unsure. That tension in the not-quite-knowing is where drama thrives.

And don't forget the environment—it should be as active a participant in the chase as the characters themselves. A storm can wash away tracks. A desert can dry up horses. A forest can hide ambushes. The West is wild for a reason. Use that to your advantage. Ask ChatGPT: *"Describe how changing terrain impacts a Western pursuit."* You'll get ideas for how to make each leg of the journey feel distinct and perilous, whether it's quicksand in the lowlands or a blizzard in the Rockies.

Characters should evolve during the chase. Every mile should strip them down, harden their resolve, or soften their hate. Maybe the pursuer begins to question their motives. Maybe the fugitive starts to feel the weight of guilt. Maybe both are chasing something inside themselves more than each other. Ask ChatGPT: *"How can a Western chase reveal character flaws and growth?"* From there, you can build internal arcs that mirror the physical journey, creating layers of tension that feed each other.

The chase also gives you the chance to experiment with narrative shifts. Maybe the story starts with the perspective of the pursuer, but halfway through, you flip to the point of view of the pursued. Or you split the narrative between both, showing how close—or far—they really are. This structure can build tension beautifully, especially if you use it to create misdirection. Ask ChatGPT to help structure this: *"Outline a Western chase told from alternating perspectives."* The back-and-forth dynamic creates a rhythm like a galloping horse—one beat driving into the next.

And then comes the climax. The final confrontation. This should feel inevitable, not convenient. It's the point where tension and emotion peak. The characters are exhausted, bruised, changed. And the question hangs heavy in the air: Will the chaser do what they came to do? Or has the chase changed them? Will the fugitive surrender, fight, or beg for mercy? This isn't just the end of the chase—it's the moment of truth. Use ChatGPT to explore different endings: *"Give me three emotional outcomes for a Western standoff after a long pursuit."* You'll see how your story can break in different directions depending on who your characters have become.

Finally, don't rush the aftermath. After the dust settles, there's always something left unsaid. Regret. Relief. Emptiness. Let it breathe. Show the cost of the chase, not just the result. Maybe the hero wins, but it doesn't feel like a victory. Maybe the fugitive escapes, but the chaser finds peace anyway. That final note is what sticks with the reader. And that's what gives your chase meaning beyond motion.

Writing a chase in a Western drama isn't about speed—it's about stakes. It's about what each character is running from, what they're chasing, and how far they'll go before they fall. With ChatGPT at your side, you can test every path, build every twist, and shape the journey until it doesn't just gallop—it resonates.

So saddle up, tighten the reins, and let the chase begin. Because out in the West, you don't just run—you reveal. And what your characters reveal during the chase might be the very soul of your story.

Horses, Dust, and Six-Shooters: Building Authentic Scenes

If you want your Western drama to leap off the page or screen, you have to get the little things right—the creak of leather, the crunch of dry earth under boots, the gleam of a polished six-shooter catching the late afternoon sun. These details don't just make your world believable—they make it *feel* alive. You can have the most compelling characters and the richest plot, but if your scenes don't breathe authenticity, they'll feel like stage sets instead of places your audience can step into. Horses, dust, and six-shooters aren't just props. They're part of the rhythm, atmosphere, and poetry of the West.

The West isn't clean. It's rugged, rough, and unfiltered. When you build a scene, don't imagine a movie set—imagine a place where the air smells like sweat, tobacco, and gun oil. That's where your characters live. A saloon isn't just a place to drink—it's where secrets are whispered, fights are started, and deals are made. The general store isn't just where folks buy flour—it's where grudges simmer and the past stares you down from across the room. Ask ChatGPT: *"Describe a saloon in a remote Western town during a dust storm."* Let the AI paint the picture, then layer in your own grit. Don't just see the room—*feel* it.

One of the quickest ways to build realism is to know your gear. Westerns aren't just about people—they're about tools, weapons, animals, and landscapes. When someone draws a six-shooter, it should feel real. There's weight, tension, and muscle memory involved. Ask ChatGPT: *"Describe how it feels to draw a Colt Single Action Army revolver from a worn leather holster."* You'll get not just the technical movement, but the emotional and sensory weight of the action. That's where authenticity lives. It's not in the facts—it's in the *feeling* of the facts.

And don't forget the horses. Horses aren't cars. They're characters, companions, and survival tools all wrapped in muscle and instinct. A Western without believable horses is like a song with no rhythm. Ask ChatGPT: *"Describe a relationship between a cowboy and his aging horse."* You might get tenderness, tension, and years of history in one brief exchange. A horse reacts to gunfire, to terrain, to the rider's nerves. You don't just ride a horse—you bond with it, rely on it, talk to it in ways only the two of you understand.

Dust is another character in your story. It clings to the boots, stings the eyes, fills the lungs. It makes people irritable, uncomfortable, and tired. A good dust storm can be more threatening than a villain, and a long ride through dry country can become a test of spirit. Ask ChatGPT: *"Write a scene where two outlaws camp for the night in a dust-blown canyon."* You'll find mood, atmosphere, and weariness woven into every word. The dust isn't just a setting—it's pressure, a reminder of the harsh world your characters live in.

Your Western scenes should also carry tension, even in the quiet moments. A man sharpening a knife. A woman sitting still, watching strangers come into town. A child holding their breath while two riders pass. These moments don't need dialogue—they need detail. What does the light look like? What's that sound in the distance? Who notices who first? Use ChatGPT to help you ask better questions: *"Describe the quiet before a gunfight in a Western town."* Let that silence speak.

And when it comes to six-shooters, remember that every shot has a purpose. Bullets aren't infinite. Guns misfire. Recoil kicks. A quick draw is as much about nerve as it is about speed. Gunfights should be messy, desperate, and personal. Ask ChatGPT: *"Describe a realistic gunfight in a narrow alley between a sheriff and a fugitive."* What you get will help you choreograph not just the action, but the emotion. Is it vengeance? Fear? Panic? Regret? Make sure your characters aren't just pulling triggers—they're making choices.

Another layer to add is the effect of the scene on your characters. Did the dust get into someone's wound? Did the horse refuse to ride further, forcing a change in plans? Did the echo of a single gunshot in the canyon bring lawmen from miles away? Nothing should happen in isolation. Every scene should leave a mark on someone or something. That's how your story stays alive—through consequences.

You can also use ChatGPT to add cultural and environmental texture. Ask: *"What kind of food would be cooking over a fire in a cattle drive camp?"* or *"What did settlers use to treat a snakebite in the 1870s?"* These small details make your world feel lived-in. They're not exposition—they're flavor. Sprinkle them into scenes like spice, and suddenly your Western isn't just believable—it's immersive.

And remember—don't rush your descriptions. Let the reader or viewer sit in the saddle a bit. Feel the leather groan. Watch the buzzards circle. Smell the gunpowder. Writing authentic scenes means slowing down when it matters, zooming in when something's at stake. ChatGPT can help you stretch those moments. Ask for variations. Ask for alternatives. Say: *"Give me three ways to describe a tense standoff at sunset."* Then pick the one that makes your pulse jump.

Your job as a writer is to make the West feel real—not like a postcard, but like a place where people live, struggle, and bleed. Horses, dust, and six-shooters aren't just part of the genre—they're the language of it. Use them with care. Use them with confidence. And use them with purpose.

Because when your scenes feel authentic, your story doesn't just entertain—it *transports*. And that's what the Western does best. It takes you somewhere raw, beautiful, and unforgiving. A place where every scene is a test. A place where survival is earned, and legends are written in dust and blood.

Setting the Scene: Saloon, Jailhouse, and Sunset

Western drama lives and dies by its sense of place. You can write a gripping story with memorable characters and sharp dialogue, but if your scenes don't feel anchored in a believable world, it'll all fall apart like a tent in the wind. The West isn't just a backdrop—it's a living, breathing world that shapes your characters, their choices, and the very tone of your story. And within that world, a few classic locations always carry more weight than others. The saloon, the jailhouse, and the sunset—they aren't just familiar images. They're storytelling tools. Symbols. Mood-setters. Each one offers a space to reveal character, heighten tension, and wrap the audience in the feel of the frontier.

Let's start with the saloon. It's the beating heart of the town, a place of chaos and commerce, sin and salvation. It's where cowboys blow their wages, where outlaws disappear into the crowd, and where the piano plays just loud enough to cover the sound of trouble brewing in the corner. When you write a saloon scene, don't just describe the swinging doors and a few bottles of whiskey. Feel the heat of bodies packed close, the dusty boots stomping across warped floorboards, the tension hanging in the air like smoke.

Use ChatGPT to build it out. Ask: *"Describe a crowded saloon during a hot Western night."* You'll get a room full of energy, movement, and underlying threat. Maybe there's a man in the corner nobody recognizes. Maybe the bartender knows who he is but isn't saying. Maybe the regulars sense it too, and that shifts the whole atmosphere. The saloon becomes a stage for more than drinking—it becomes a theater of unspoken truths, power plays, and past sins resurfacing. Even a quiet drink at the bar can be a loaded moment if you frame it right.

Now, shift to the jailhouse. The jail isn't just a holding cell—it's where the rules get tested. It's where the lawman draws the line, and the outlaw dares him to cross it. The jailhouse in a Western story should never feel like a safe place. It's filled with the threat of escape, of mob justice, of internal conflict. Maybe the sheriff locks a man up but doubts his guilt. Maybe the town wants blood and the jail becomes a last stand. Or maybe the prisoner is the one telling the truth, and the real villain holds the keys.

You can use ChatGPT to push this tension further. Ask: *"Describe a jailhouse in a Western town on the verge of a lynch mob."* What you get won't just be a room with bars—it'll be pressure in the air, the creak of the wooden floor as the sheriff paces, the glow of lantern light flickering against faces outside the window. The jailhouse becomes a crucible, a place where character is tested and the consequences of every decision ring louder than gunfire. It's the last place where the law still means something—or where it finally breaks.

And then there's the sunset. It might seem like a cliché, but in a Western, the sunset means everything. It's not just beautiful—it's symbolic. It signals the end of something. A life, a day, a chapter, a dream. It marks the passing of time in a place where time itself feels slower but more meaningful. A character riding into the sunset isn't just leaving town—they're leaving behind what they were. Or maybe they're going somewhere they can't return from. The sunset is mood, closure, melancholy. It's a farewell written in light.

Try this with ChatGPT: *"Write a scene where two former friends sit quietly and watch the sunset after a standoff."* The silence will speak volumes. Maybe they don't say much. Maybe one of them knows he won't be alive when the sun rises. That golden light becomes more than scenery—it becomes emotion. A kind of farewell without needing to say goodbye. And it works whether it's hopeful, bitter, or ambiguous.

You can use the three locations together for powerful storytelling arcs. The saloon for temptation, chaos, or unexpected reunions. The jailhouse for justice, judgment, or the last threads of loyalty. And the sunset for closure, transformation, or the calm before the storm. Think of them as emotional markers. A saloon scene might open your story with bravado and tension. The jailhouse might sit in the middle of your narrative, tightening the screws. And the sunset might cap a moment of deep change—a character letting go of vengeance, or finally embracing it.

These spaces also work to reveal sides of your characters they might try to hide. A gunfighter might bluff and joke in the saloon but go quiet and vulnerable behind the bars. A bounty hunter might show no mercy during the day but watch the sunset with something close to regret. Ask ChatGPT: *"How can setting reflect a character's internal change in a Western?"* You'll see how the world becomes a mirror. When used with intention, the setting does more than hold the story—it *tells* it.

Atmosphere matters. It's not enough for your readers or audience to see the West—they need to *feel* it. They need to hear the clink of glasses, smell the sweat and smoke, sense the building dread as the sun drops behind the hills. When you use these iconic settings with purpose, you're not just honoring the tradition of the Western—you're adding depth to it.

And when you're stuck, use ChatGPT to keep the mood flowing. Ask for variations: *"Give me three versions of a saloon scene, one light-hearted, one suspenseful, and one tragic."* You'll see how even the same setting can play completely differently depending on tone, character, and intention.

So when you set the scene in your Western, don't just drop your characters into a dusty room and hope it works. Let the saloon breathe, let the jailhouse press in, and let the sunset say everything your characters can't. Build it with detail. Infuse it with purpose. And always remember—the West is more than a place. It's a state of mind.

The Role of Nature in Western Storytelling

Nature isn't just the setting in a Western—it's a character in its own right. It's vast, unpredictable, beautiful, and brutal. It shapes the people who ride through it, tests them, humbles them, and sometimes claims them. The wide-open plains, jagged mountain ranges, bone-dry deserts, and violent storms don't just provide a backdrop for your drama—they *are* the drama. In Western storytelling, nature is both enemy and ally, offering escape, isolation, or death, depending on who your character is and how they treat the land. And when you're writing your Western with ChatGPT, you've got a tool that can help you harness the wild in all its forms.

Start by recognizing that the land sets the tone. A story that takes place in a wind-blasted canyon full of rattlesnakes is going to feel very different from one set in a lush, high-elevation valley after a heavy rain. Every hill, gulch, river, and mesa tells its own story. You can use nature to reflect your characters' inner world. Ask ChatGPT: *"Describe a scene in which a dying outlaw crosses a barren salt flat."* What you get won't just be about terrain—it will be about mood, suffering, and isolation. The land becomes a mirror, echoing every cough, limp, or thought of regret.

Nature is a test of endurance. In the West, survival is never guaranteed, no matter how tough your character is. You can use the environment to push your characters physically and emotionally. Maybe your hero has to cross a desert with a wounded companion and one canteen of water. Maybe your fugitive flees into the snowy Rockies with a posse on his trail and a storm coming in. These aren't just logistical obstacles—they're pressure points. They force choices. They reveal what kind of person your character really is. Ask ChatGPT: *"What happens to a lone rider during a sudden thunderstorm on the prairie?"* You'll get wind, lightning, soaked gunpowder, and a whole lot of tension to play with.

Nature also forces stillness, and that's a gift in Western storytelling. A man stranded without a horse might sit by a dried creek bed and reckon with everything he's done. A woman watching the sunrise from a canyon edge might have a moment of clarity that changes the course of her journey. These quiet moments aren't filler. They're the soul of your story. ChatGPT can help you find them. Ask: *"Write a reflective scene where a character watches the sun rise over the desert after a night of violence."* You'll find poetry, regret, and maybe even hope hidden in the horizon.

Don't forget how nature shapes your characters' behavior and worldview. A man who grew up in the mountains is going to think and speak differently than someone raised in the dust bowl of West Texas. Their values, their toughness, their knowledge of the land all come from where they've survived. Use ChatGPT to explore this: *"Describe how a character raised in the Wyoming wilderness sees the world."* The more tied your character is to the land, the more grounded and believable they'll feel.

And then there's the symbolic power of nature. The desert is often used to represent emptiness, both spiritual and emotional. The forest can represent the unknown or a return to primal instincts. Rivers are often tied to cleansing or rebirth. The mountain? That's the great test, the place one climbs to find truth—or to die trying. These symbols aren't subtle, but in Westerns, they don't have to be. You can lean into them. Ask ChatGPT: *"Give me three symbolic meanings of a canyon in a Western story."* You might get isolation, danger, and the echo of lost voices. Use these layers to deepen your scenes and give weight to the landscape.

Nature also controls time in the West. The rising and setting sun dictates travel. The seasons determine survival. Winter is deadly. Summer is merciless. Spring brings change. Fall carries decay. You can use these elements to frame your narrative. Maybe your character has until the first snowfall to settle a debt. Maybe the monsoon season is the only time the outlaw can sneak across the border. Ask ChatGPT: *"How can the changing seasons affect the plot of a Western drama?"* and you'll find structure where you might have seen only scenery.

Animals, too, are part of the natural story. Not just horses, but wolves, coyotes, vultures, rattlesnakes. They can be omens, threats, or even companions. A buzzard circling overhead can say more than a paragraph of exposition. A coyote's howl can signal loneliness, danger, or freedom. Ask ChatGPT: *"Write a scene where a cowboy wakes to find a wolf staring at him across the fire."* You'll get a moment thick with primal tension, something that ties your character to the natural world in a way no line of dialogue could.

Nature can also act as a boundary—literally and metaphorically. A river separates one life from another. A cliff edge offers a choice: jump, fall, or turn back. A vast stretch of desert might promise freedom but demand a price. You can build entire character arcs around these confrontations with the land. A man might cross a mountain range and never come back the same. A woman might brave a desert alone to prove she doesn't need anyone else. ChatGPT can help you frame these turning points: *"Describe a scene where crossing a dangerous terrain symbolizes a character's transformation."*

In the end, Western storytelling without nature is like a gun without bullets. You need the land. You need the dust, the wind, the heat, the silence. You need the long ride under a blood-orange sky, the sound of boots on cracked earth, the buzz of flies around a still body. These are not just details—they are the pulse of your story.

So when you write, write with the land in your bones. Let the West shape your characters, your pacing, your atmosphere. Use ChatGPT to explore every hill, river, and trail until your world feels as real as the grit on your character's hands. Because in a true Western, the land isn't just where the story happens—it *is* the story. And when you get it right, the land will speak for itself.

Love on the Frontier: Romance Amidst the Dust

Romance in a Western isn't about candlelit dinners or love letters sealed with wax. It's about stolen glances by a campfire, whispered confessions under a wide-open sky, and hearts that dare to hope in a world built on hardship. Love on the frontier is raw, restrained, and rugged—carved out of loneliness, forged in survival, and as unpredictable as a desert storm. It's not the center of the story, but it can become the soul of it. When you get it right, romance in a Western drama doesn't soften the story—it deepens it, grounding the characters in something human while the wild world roars around them.

In the West, people don't fall in love with ease. There's no luxury of time, no guarantee of tomorrow. Romance grows slowly, like a stubborn seed in dry soil. It often starts with mutual respect or wary trust. A man offers to help repair a broken wagon. A woman covers a stranger's wound in silence. Neither says much, but something passes between them—something the story doesn't have to shout out loud. And that's the secret. Western love isn't loud. It simmers. It holds its breath. And when it finally breaks through, it does so with the force of everything that's been held back.

To start building this kind of romance with ChatGPT, don't ask for a love story. Ask for tension. Ask for moments that almost become something else. Try: *"Describe the first time a weary gunslinger and a ranch widow speak to each other during a supply run."* You won't get declarations of love. You'll get glances, subtext, guarded words. And that's where the real power of frontier romance lies—not in what's said, but in what isn't.

Love on the frontier is born out of circumstance. Maybe they're forced to travel together, stuck in a snowstorm or crossing outlaw country. Maybe they're both running from something—different roads, same direction. These stories grow out of survival, out of shared moments under pressure. ChatGPT can help shape these situations: *"Create a scenario where two people on opposite sides of the law are forced to rely on each other."* You'll get conflict, trust issues, and sparks that don't have to be spoken aloud to be felt.

And this love doesn't have to be perfect. In fact, it rarely is. A cowboy who's lost too much may never be able to fully open up. A woman who's survived alone might not trust easily. Maybe they both want something simple, but the world won't let them have it. These rough edges make their connection feel earned. Ask ChatGPT: *"Describe a scene where a woman who runs a waystation tends to a wounded outlaw she doesn't know whether to trust."* The tension there—between care and caution, warmth and fear—is where frontier love blooms.

You can also use love to show vulnerability in otherwise hardened characters. A stoic sheriff who barely speaks might soften when he sees her reading alone on the porch. An outlaw might risk his life not for gold, but to keep someone safe. Love becomes the one thing that makes them hesitate, and in the West, hesitation can mean life or death. That contradiction adds weight to the romance. Ask ChatGPT: *"What would make a notorious gunfighter put down his weapon for someone he loves?"* The answers you get will not only shape your love story, but your character's entire arc.

And this kind of romance doesn't always end in a happy ride into the sunset. Sometimes, love is fleeting. Sometimes it's a moment in time—a dance in a barn, a shared drink under the stars, a goodbye whispered before dawn. It might be the promise of a future that never comes. Or it might be the reason someone decides to stop running. Use ChatGPT to explore possibilities: *"List emotional outcomes of a romance between a drifter and a frontier schoolteacher."* You might find tragedy, peace, longing, or change. Whatever path you choose, let it be honest to the world your story lives in.

Love also gives you contrast. A quiet scene between two people holding hands at the edge of a canyon can hit harder than a gunfight if you've built that connection right. In a world of violence and lawlessness, tenderness becomes a rare and powerful thing. One shared look can say what five pages of dialogue never could. Ask ChatGPT: *"Write a silent moment of connection between two characters who haven't yet confessed their feelings."* What you get will help you write scenes where the tension isn't just romantic—it's emotional, and loaded with unspoken truths.

And don't forget that romance doesn't just mean young love or new love. Maybe it's the rekindling of something thought lost. Maybe it's a widower finding a second chance. Maybe it's love born of years of quiet partnership on the trail. The West isn't just for fresh starts—it's also where the past comes back. Ask ChatGPT: *"Describe a reunion between two lovers separated by war."* That history, that ache, gives your story emotional depth and richness that readers or viewers will feel in their bones.

In a Western, love isn't safe or soft—it's a gamble. It's something you hold onto while the wind howls and the world tries to take everything from you. It's a moment of warmth in a cold land. A reason to fight. A reason to stop fighting. And when you write it with care, with restraint, and with truth, it becomes unforgettable.

So let the dust settle on the trail. Let two hands brush by accident. Let a character glance back when they said they wouldn't. Let the romance unfold not in grand gestures, but in shared moments and sacrifices. Because love on the frontier doesn't need to be loud to be powerful—it just needs to be real.

When the Past Haunts the Gunslinger

A gunslinger is never just a man with a fast draw and a quiet stare. He's a living archive of everything he's seen, done, and lost. In the Western drama, the past isn't something you leave behind—it's something that rides with you, whispering in the wind, lurking in shadows, and staring back at you from the barrel of someone else's gun. When the past haunts the gunslinger, it becomes more than backstory. It becomes fuel for the drama, the wound that won't close, the storm that never blows over. And the deeper you let that past cut, the more gripping your character becomes.

The gunslinger doesn't speak much, but he carries volumes. Every scar, every twitch, every long pause before a decision—those are conversations with ghosts. Maybe he once rode with a gang and left when they went too far. Maybe he shot a man who didn't deserve it. Maybe he walked away from the only people who ever loved him, convinced that the gun in his hand would never let them be safe. The past becomes his shadow, sometimes walking beside him, sometimes overtaking him. And with ChatGPT, you can shape this haunting in ways that hit hard without ever being melodramatic.

Start by building the moment that changed him. Ask ChatGPT: *"Describe the incident that made a gunslinger put down his guns—until now."* You'll get options: a betrayal, a massacre, a moment of mercy that cost someone else their life. Pick the one that makes your gut twist. That's the memory he wakes up thinking about. That's the voice in the back of his head every time he tightens his grip on the handle of his revolver. It's not about what he *did*—it's about what it *did to him*.

When the past haunts your gunslinger, it shows up in everything he does. He doesn't sleep well. He avoids mirrors. He has a habit he doesn't explain—like carving notches in wood or staring into the fire longer than he should. These aren't quirks. They're signs of a man at war with himself. Ask ChatGPT: *"What quiet behaviors might reveal the inner torment of a former gunslinger?"* You'll get ideas that you can sprinkle throughout your story, letting the pain seep in gradually instead of pouring it all out at once.

The past also walks into the story in the form of other people. Maybe an old enemy has tracked him down, still angry over something that happened fifteen years ago. Maybe a child shows up claiming to be his. Maybe a woman he once loved steps out of the crowd in a town he swore he'd never return to. These ghosts with names and faces are harder to ignore. They force him to confront who he was and who he still might be. You can use ChatGPT to flesh these characters out: *"Create a woman from a gunslinger's past who still loves him but doesn't trust him."* From that, entire subplots begin to take shape—ones soaked in regret, tension, and unfinished business.

And sometimes, the past isn't what he remembers—it's what he *doesn't* want to remember. Repressed trauma can make for powerful storytelling. Maybe he doesn't know why he wakes up in a cold sweat, why he drinks too much, why he can't stop running. The truth can unravel slowly, a memory at a time, until it crashes into the present. Ask ChatGPT: *"What kind of traumatic memory might a gunslinger be running from without realizing it?"* You'll get raw, vivid ideas that don't just explain behavior—they *complicate* it, deepen it, and make the character feel human.

Flashbacks, when used right, can show the weight of the past without slowing the pace. They don't need to be long. A flicker of memory during a gunfight. A voice echoing over a canyon ridge. The sound of boots on wood triggering the memory of a brother falling to the ground. These moments are quick but potent. You can ask ChatGPT to help you write them: *"Write a short flashback to a gunslinger's worst mistake during his time in a gang."* Then layer that moment into a scene where it doesn't belong—because that's how memory works. It doesn't knock. It barges in.

Sometimes the past isn't just emotional—it's following him with boots and bullets. Maybe he left someone alive who swore revenge. Maybe he took something that someone else wants back. Maybe he earned a reputation he can't shake, and every young gun in the territory wants to make a name by taking him down. That kind of past creates external conflict that feeds off internal guilt. Ask ChatGPT: *"Describe a gunslinger who's hunted by the son of a man he killed in self-defense."* That story doesn't have to be about the duel—it's about the guilt, the hesitation, and the fear of history repeating itself.

And then there's the moral question: can a man like him ever change? Does redemption even exist in a place like the frontier? Maybe he tries. Maybe he lays down his guns, takes up a trade, tries to help someone. But the past isn't always ready to let him move on. That's the emotional tension that drives many of the best Westerns—the hope of change constantly being tested by the ghosts of old choices. Ask ChatGPT: *"How might a gunslinger try to redeem himself in a Western setting?"* You'll find ideas full of struggle, sacrifice, and maybe, just maybe, salvation.

The beauty of letting the past haunt the gunslinger is that you can explore it in layers. Not every memory has to come with a big reveal. Sometimes it's a name he refuses to say. A road he won't ride down. A song he never wants to hear again. Those subtle nods to something deeper create mystery and build tension. They make your audience lean forward, wanting to know what lies beneath the silence.

In the Western, the past never stays buried. It rides in just before dusk, kicks open the saloon doors, and demands answers. It's not there for revenge—it's there for reckoning. And the gunslinger, no matter how far he's traveled, has to face it eventually.

So when you write your gunslinger, let his past speak. Let it whisper, shout, or linger in his silence. Use ChatGPT to find the cracks in his armor and fill them with dust, memory, and regret. Because a Western without a haunted man is just noise. But a story where the past rides close behind—that's where legends are born.

Writing the Wagon Trail Journey

There's something deeply mythic about the wagon trail journey. It's more than just a trek across land—it's a pilgrimage, a gamble, and often a slow unraveling of the people brave or desperate enough to make it. In Western drama, the wagon trail is a rolling crucible, where hope collides with hardship and every mile chips away at illusions. It's where families are tested, leaders rise or fall, and where nature, man, and fate all take turns deciding who survives. Writing a wagon trail journey is about capturing the rhythm of the road, the slow grind of distance, and the way the landscape becomes both a promise and a threat.

Start with what the journey means. Nobody rides a wagon for comfort. They're chasing something—land, freedom, escape, a second chance. You can use ChatGPT to explore these motivations with a prompt like: *"Describe why a widow with two children would join a wagon train west in 1865."* The story that emerges isn't just logistics—it's emotional ballast. That purpose will shape every decision she makes along the way, every risk she takes, and every moment where she falters but refuses to quit.

The wagon trail is a place where characters evolve through experience. The kid who started out wide-eyed and reckless might learn hard lessons about responsibility and loss. The cynical scout might rediscover faith in people. The quiet farmer might be forced to kill for the first time. Each moment on the trail should either test, transform, or tear down. With ChatGPT, you can map that out: *"What are key character development moments during a wagon train journey?"* Use those suggestions to weave your arcs through the dust and danger.

Setting up your caravan of wagons also opens the door for ensemble storytelling. You're not following one man on a horse—you're following a whole slice of humanity inching its way west. Different people, different agendas, different backgrounds, all trapped in the same slow-moving crucible. Ask ChatGPT to help build this community: *"Create five wagon trail characters with conflicting goals."* Then let those goals clash. Someone's in it for land, someone for religion, someone's running from the law. That friction is where drama lives.

Pacing the journey is crucial. A wagon trail story doesn't gallop—it trudges. There's monotony. Long stretches of sameness broken by moments of shock. A river crossing that goes wrong. A storm that scatters the wagons. A child falls sick. A wheel breaks. These incidents aren't interruptions—they're part of the rhythm. They shape the trail like storms shape a coastline. Ask ChatGPT: *"What are realistic hazards faced on a wagon trail in 19th-century America?"* You'll get everything from cholera to stampedes, and you can build these into turning points that push the story forward.

Nature is a relentless character on the wagon trail. The land isn't passive. It burns, freezes, floods, and fights back. Heat makes tempers short. Dust clouds kill visibility and morale. Thunderstorms keep the wagons bogged in mud for days. When writing these scenes, go beyond weather reports—make the land emotional. Ask ChatGPT: *"Describe a wagon train's struggle during a sandstorm in the plains."* Let it be chaotic, sensory, and exhausting. Let it change someone for good.

Tension on the trail isn't always external. Sometimes the danger is within. Maybe there's a traitor among the travelers. Maybe someone's stealing supplies. Maybe two men are in love with the same woman. A wagon trail becomes a pressure cooker. What starts as cooperation can curdle into suspicion, jealousy, even murder. Ask ChatGPT to build on this: *"Describe a growing conflict between a wagon master and a wealthy settler."* That conflict can simmer, flare up, and eventually explode at the worst possible moment.

And then there are the quiet moments—sunset meals cooked over a fire, a fiddle tune played beneath a canopy of stars, a father teaching his son to shoot, a mother braiding her daughter's hair for what might be the last time. These scenes make the hardship worth it. They remind the audience what's at stake. You can ask ChatGPT: *"Write a quiet moment of hope on a wagon trail after a tragedy."* The stillness and reflection between disasters are just as powerful as the action.

Romance on the trail also has a raw honesty to it. There's no time for long courtships. Love on the trail is built in glances, shared water, a steadying hand during a river crossing. It's whispered promises made in wagons, hurried kisses under blankets, and silent support when words fall short. It's not always meant to last—but while it lasts, it matters. You can ask ChatGPT to help shape these bonds: *"Describe a growing romance between two people traveling the Oregon Trail."* The answers will help you capture love in the margins of struggle.

As your characters reach the final leg of the journey, they should be different. Maybe they've lost loved ones. Maybe they've buried their former selves. Maybe what they find at the end of the trail isn't what they expected—or wanted. But that's part of what gives the wagon trail its power. It's not about reaching the destination. It's about surviving the road. Ask ChatGPT: *"How should a wagon trail story end for maximum emotional impact?"* You might get ideas involving homecoming, disillusionment, death, or the quiet triumph of those who simply endured.

And don't forget the symbolism of the trail itself. It represents change. It represents the great unknown. It's a road with no guarantees, paved in loss and possibility. Every bump, every night spent under open sky, every grave dug in roadside soil—they all leave their mark.

So when you write the wagon trail, don't rush it. Let the pace reflect the burden. Let the landscape challenge, the people unravel, the stakes rise with every mile. Use ChatGPT to help you populate the trail with voices, trials, secrets, and moments of grace. Because the wagon trail isn't just a road across a map. It's a journey through character, sacrifice, and what it really means to keep going—when the wheels break, the oxen collapse, and hope is hanging by a thread.

That's not just a journey. That's Western drama at its most human.

The Gold Rush: Greed, Glory, and Great Stories

The Gold Rush was the spark that set half the country on fire with dreams of wealth, freedom, and reinvention. It drew in every kind of person you can imagine—farm boys, gamblers, ex-soldiers, desperate men, wild women, freed slaves, immigrants, and swindlers—and it dropped them all into camps and hills where law meant little, and fortune meant everything. In Western drama, the Gold Rush isn't just an era—it's a furnace. It burns away pretence, reveals what people are really made of, and gives you everything you need to build stories full of conflict, ambition, betrayal, and survival. It's where greed collides with hope, and glory dances just out of reach.

Writing a Western set during the Gold Rush gives you one of the richest storytelling backdrops imaginable. You're not just writing about gold—you're writing about obsession. The moment a character sees their first fleck of gold glittering in a pan, they change. It awakens something primal. Some get hungry, some get scared, and some get mean. You can ask ChatGPT: *"Describe the psychological impact of striking gold for the first time."* You'll find yourself staring at the beginnings of a character arc built not just on success but on the weight of what that success does to a person.

The Gold Rush also lets you explore all the social layers that crossed paths on the frontier. Chinese workers driven from their homeland by poverty, Irish immigrants fleeing famine, freed slaves seeking land and dignity, and women who realized they could earn in a mining town what no man would have paid them back East. These people didn't just dig in the dirt—they built the West with blood and calluses. Use ChatGPT to create these characters: *"Describe a diverse group of people in a California gold mining camp in 1850."* You'll get a rich ensemble, each with a different dream, and each bound to clash when gold becomes scarce.

At the core of every Gold Rush story is the question of *what are you willing to do to strike it rich?* That's where the drama lives. Two friends who set out together, but only one comes back. A woman who claims a dead man's claim as her own. A prospector who hides his find, only to be murdered in the night. These stories don't need to be dressed up with plot twists. The setting *is* the twist. Every moment holds the potential for betrayal. Ask ChatGPT: *"Create a plot where two gold miners discover a rich vein and turn on each other."* You'll find all the bones of a powerful Western tragedy.

The environment also plays a crucial role in Gold Rush storytelling. You're not writing in a saloon or jailhouse now—you're in the mountains, the canyons, the freezing rivers. Nature doesn't care how rich you are. The winters are brutal. The rivers flood. The land slides. The food runs out. Disease spreads fast. When you add nature's indifference to human greed, you get powerful scenes where the land becomes the final judge. Use ChatGPT: *"Describe the hardships of living in a remote gold mining camp during a harsh winter."* That kind of detail builds more than setting—it builds dread.

You can also use the Gold Rush to explore ambition versus morality. Maybe your protagonist is a good man who finds a fortune but doesn't want to become like the animals around him. Maybe he has to decide whether to keep the gold or use it to save a rival's life. Maybe he loses everything because he refused to steal, and we're left wondering if that makes him a fool or a hero. That's the heart of a great Western—putting good people in bad situations and watching which part of them survives. Ask ChatGPT: *"What moral dilemmas might arise for a prospector who discovers gold near a starving settlement?"* You'll find storylines layered with complexity.

There's also plenty of room for power dynamics and manipulation. Maybe the town banker is buying up failed claims for pennies, knowing full well there's gold under them. Maybe a preacher uses fear of damnation to take a cut from every pan. Maybe a saloon owner runs the whole camp from behind her bar. These are your power players, and gold is their currency of control. Use ChatGPT: *"Create a character who uses the Gold Rush to build an empire without ever lifting a pickaxe."* That kind of villain is perfect for a slow burn plot, quietly corrupting everything around them until the whole town stinks of greed.

Of course, not all stories have to be grim. There's also room for glory—for the lucky strike, the big win, the underdog who makes it and doesn't sell their soul in the process. Maybe someone uses their gold to build something good. Maybe they return home, not richer in money, but in perspective. The Gold Rush doesn't just test people—it changes them. Ask ChatGPT: *"Describe a miner who gives away his fortune and why."* That choice might define your theme: that some things are worth more than gold, and some people only discover that after they've lost it all.

The sensory detail in Gold Rush storytelling is golden too. The clink of pickaxes. The icy sting of mountain rivers. The sour smell of unwashed bodies packed into tents. The glitter of fool's gold that shatters a man's hope. Use those textures. Make your scenes visceral. Ask ChatGPT: *"Write a descriptive paragraph set in a noisy mining camp at night."* You'll feel the grit, the desperation, and maybe even the flicker of a dream someone refuses to let go of.

And finally, don't forget the legacy of gold. The towns that boomed and died. The land torn up and left to rot. The families made and broken. The men who struck it rich and lost their souls. The women who came west looking for opportunity and found only survival. The Gold Rush left more than gold behind—it left stories. And those stories are yours to tell.

So dig deep. Let your characters dream big, fall hard, and claw their way through mud, lies, and longing. Use ChatGPT to help shape the stakes, sculpt the personalities, and let the gold shine just enough to blind—but never enough to hide the truth underneath.

Because in a Western drama, the Gold Rush isn't just a chapter in history. It's a mirror held up to the human heart—and what it's willing to risk for the promise of more.

Using ChatGPT to Create a Cast of Gritty Characters

Western drama thrives on grit—characters who are flawed, weather-worn, complex, and as unpredictable as the land they live on. These aren't people who smile for the camera or deliver polished speeches. They spit dust, carry grudges, and walk through fire with cracked boots and heavier souls. Whether you're writing a lonely drifter, a scarred sheriff, a grieving widow, or a two-bit thief with a golden heart, the real strength of your Western story comes from the humanity under all that grit. And with ChatGPT, you've got a tool that can help you build these characters from the boots up.

Creating gritty characters doesn't mean making them angry or foul-mouthed—it means giving them pasts that hurt, choices that cost, and lives that haven't been easy. You start with their wounds. What did they survive? What did they lose? What do they refuse to talk about but can't stop carrying? Prompt ChatGPT with: *"Create a former Civil War scout who lost everything and now works as a blacksmith."* The reply won't just give you a job description—it'll offer scars, regrets, maybe even a buried talent or secret kindness. That's the heart of grit: strength tempered by suffering.

You can go deeper by asking about personality through behavior. Try: *"What quiet habits might reveal the past of a tough Western saloonkeeper who used to be an outlaw?"* You'll get details like how they clean the same glass over and over when nervous, or why they never sit with their back to the door. These aren't just cool quirks. They're windows into a life lived hard—and a mind that's always watching the exits.

To build out a well-rounded cast, ask ChatGPT for archetypes with a twist. You don't want cardboard cut-outs—you want people who fit the world but surprise the audience. Prompt it with: *"Give me five gritty Western characters, each with a secret they're hiding."* You might get a traveling preacher who used to run with a gang, a young ranch hand who can't read but dreams of writing a book, or a bounty hunter with a bounty on his own head. Each one is a seed for drama, tension, and revelation.

Relationships also define grit. Who do your characters trust? Who do they hate? Who have they buried? You can ask ChatGPT: *"Describe the dynamic between a veteran sheriff and his impulsive deputy who may be his illegitimate son."* That alone sets up conflict, loyalty, emotional baggage, and the kind of unresolved tension that makes scenes crackle even when no one draws a gun.

And don't forget the women of the West—who were often tougher, smarter, and more resourceful than the men they outlived. Ask ChatGPT to help you break stereotypes: *"Create a gritty female character in a Western who runs a freight business and carries a shotgun."* You'll get someone who doesn't need rescuing, who's seen every kind of lie a man can tell, and who doesn't trust anyone who smiles too easily. These characters don't just survive—they run the show.

ChatGPT can also help you build characters with moral complexity. The best Westerns aren't about good vs. evil—they're about hard choices in a hard world. Try: *"Create a conflicted outlaw who robs from railroads but gives money to struggling townsfolk."* Now you've got someone the reader doesn't know whether to love or fear. The tension that comes from that confusion is what makes a character stick long after the story ends.

If you want grit in dialogue, you can ask ChatGPT for voice. Try: *"Give me a short exchange between a gambler and a sheriff in a tense saloon scene."* Let the words do the heavy lifting. Let the pauses, insults, and loaded silences reveal character more than exposition ever could. A gritty character says little, but everything they say cuts to the bone.

You can even create contrast within the cast to bring out the grit. A naive settler walking into a town run by cynical survivors. A young schoolteacher crossing paths with a man who hasn't spoken to a child in ten years. These juxtapositions create opportunity—for conflict, humor, or even unexpected compassion. Ask: *"Create a group of characters traveling together on a dangerous trail, each with different motivations."* You'll get a walking powder keg of tension and story potential.

Grit also comes from how characters handle loss and danger. Some run. Some laugh in the face of it. Some go silent and do what needs doing. Ask ChatGPT: *"How might different characters react to the death of someone in their group on a cattle drive?"* One might cry, one might get drunk, one might bury the body with care and say nothing. Those reactions tell you everything.

When writing your cast, don't chase perfection. Chase truth. The West wasn't clean, and neither were its people. They cheated, they lied, they fought, they loved, and they kept going even when everything hurt. That's what makes them compelling. With ChatGPT, you can refine these personalities, test their limits, throw them into trouble, and watch what comes out the other side.

So build your cast with calluses, regrets, nicknames, secrets, and scars. Give them reasons to stay, reasons to run, and reasons to draw steel. Let them surprise you. Let them surprise each other. Because in a Western, grit isn't just toughness—it's survival. And survival always makes for a hell of a good story.

Bibles, Booze, and Bullets: Everyday Life in the 1800s

The American West in the 1800s wasn't all duels at high noon and gold strikes in the riverbeds. Most of it was spent doing the hard, slow, dirty work of surviving. Everyday life was a grinding mix of hope, habit, and hardship, where the only certainties were dust, danger, and the need to keep moving forward. When you're writing Western drama, especially using a tool like ChatGPT, grounding your story in the mundane reality of the 19th century can make your world breathe with authenticity. And sometimes, the ordinary—when sharpened with detail and pressure—becomes more dramatic than the shootouts.

Let's start with the three things that framed most people's lives in the West: Bibles, booze, and bullets. These weren't just props—they were systems of belief, comfort, and survival.

The Bible sat on nearly every table, even if the folks living under that roof were far from saintly. Religion gave people order in a place that often had none. Preachers rode circuits, delivering sermons in saloons or under the open sky, and even the most hardened gunman might whisper a prayer before a gunfight or a drink. Ask ChatGPT: *"Describe how religion shaped the daily life of a frontier woman raising five children alone."* You'll get insight into the quiet strength that often held communities together, even as violence circled the town like buzzards.

Booze was the frontier's medicine, social glue, and curse. Whiskey flowed through mining camps, cattle towns, and backroom poker games. It fueled friendships and feuds alike. Some drank to celebrate, some drank to forget, and some drank because the water wasn't fit for a horse. A saloon wasn't just a watering hole—it was often the town's first building, a gathering place where news traveled faster than the telegraph. Ask ChatGPT to describe a typical night in a saloon, and you'll get laughter, fistfights, business deals, and broken dreams—all under one creaky roof.

And then there were the bullets. Guns weren't ornamental. They were tools, just like axes or spades, and most everyone knew how to use them. Whether it was a revolver on the hip or a rifle hanging by the door, firepower meant protection from rustlers, bandits, or wild animals. Shooting contests, target practice, and hunting were part of daily life, not just something that came with trouble. Ask ChatGPT: *"Describe a morning hunting trip between a father and his teenage son in 1870s Montana."* You'll get the rhythm of normalcy—a kind of peace that existed right alongside violence.

But life wasn't all grit and gunpowder. There were dances held in barns, schoolhouses with chalk and slates, laundry days by the creek, and long walks to pick wildflowers. People courted each other slowly, wrote letters that took weeks to arrive, and cooked everything from scratch. A meal wasn't just a necessity—it was an event. You can ask ChatGPT: *"What would a pioneer family eat for supper in a sod house during winter?"* and get recipes steeped in hardship and ingenuity—rabbit stew, cornbread, canned peaches if they were lucky.

Trade and barter ran many towns. If you didn't have money, you offered what you could—eggs, sewing work, help with harvest. Everyone had a skill. Blacksmiths, farriers, coopers, carpenters, and midwives were vital. Children helped with chores. Women managed homes, livestock, and sometimes the businesses too. Towns weren't just groups of buildings—they were webs of obligation, suspicion, and interdependence. You could ask ChatGPT to help design a community: *"Create a small frontier town and list ten key residents and their roles."* What you'll get is more than names—you'll get tension, gossip, loyalty, and history baked into the land.

Clothing was durable and sparse. People wore what worked. A cowboy might wear the same duster every day for years. A woman might have one good dress and a patched-up work outfit. Children often wore hand-me-downs, and boots were a prized possession. Hygiene was minimal by modern standards, but that didn't mean people didn't care. Bathing was a luxury, shaving a skill, and barbers often doubled as dentists. A scene where a man shaves in silence before a duel can be filled with meaning. Ask ChatGPT: *"Describe the act of shaving with a straight razor before a gunfight."* You'll find layers in even the smallest actions.

Communication was slow and uncertain. News came by telegraph or word of mouth. Rumors spread like wildfire, and misinformation could get someone killed. A wanted poster might be weeks out of date. Letters were precious, read and reread until the paper wore thin. You can use ChatGPT to capture that sense of isolation: *"Write a scene where a young wife receives a long-awaited letter from her husband on the trail."* It's not just about the message—it's about the weight of time and silence between the lines.

Travel was grueling. Wagons broke down, horses went lame, and trails could disappear in a storm. Most people didn't ride off into the sunset—they trudged through mud, snow, or dry heat, sometimes walking alongside their wagons to save the animals. Ask ChatGPT: *"Describe a family's travel day along the Oregon Trail."* You'll get creaky wheels, blistered feet, singing to pass the time, and the quiet tension of watching the horizon for signs of danger.

And then there was entertainment. A fiddle, a deck of cards, a tall tale, or a poem recited from memory by the fire. People told stories because stories were how they remembered who they were. And when the work was done—when the horses were stabled, the children asleep, and the fire low—that was when the storytelling began. That's when legends were born, not with bullets, but with words.

Everyday life in the 1800s wasn't glamorous, but it was rich with detail, routine, and moments of grit and grace. When you're using ChatGPT to bring it all to life, don't just ask for action scenes. Ask for what people did when nothing was happening. Ask for what they feared when the night got too quiet. Ask for what they hoped for when all they had was prayer and persistence.

Because Western drama isn't just about the moments that make history—it's about the lives people lived in between. That's where the truth is. That's where your story breathes.

Dialogue with a Drawl: Talking like a Westerner

There's nothing that roots a Western story more firmly in its world than the way its characters talk. Western dialogue has a sound all its own—slow in rhythm, heavy with subtext, plainspoken, but always charged with more than the words let on. It's not just what they say—it's how they say it. That dusty drawl, that careful choice of words, that tendency to let silence say more than speech—that's what gives Western drama its soul. Getting the dialogue right doesn't mean packing every sentence with slang or cliché—it means understanding the voice of the land, the time, and the people hardened by both.

Writing Western dialogue is a balancing act between authenticity and clarity. You want that country rhythm and grit without turning your story into a caricature. A little goes a long way. Ask ChatGPT something like: *"Write a conversation between a sheriff and a ranch hand about a missing horse, using 1870s frontier dialect."* What you'll get isn't just dialogue—it's tone, rhythm, and the unspoken rules of how people spoke to each other in a world where words were often chosen with care.

A Westerner doesn't waste breath. Their sentences are shorter, tighter. They talk like folks who know silence better than they know speech. When someone says something, it usually matters. They don't dress up their feelings in poetry. They bury them in understatement. Instead of saying "I'm afraid I might die," a Westerner might say, "Ain't feelin' lucky today." Instead of "I love you," it might just be, "I reckon I'd miss you somethin' fierce." It's what they don't say that lingers longest.

Tone often comes from pacing. Western dialogue tends to stretch out, not in length, but in rhythm. There are pauses. There's hesitation. There are long looks and longer silences between the words. That drawl isn't just accent—it's attitude. A man might say "Mornin'" with a tip of his hat and say more than a paragraph ever could. Ask ChatGPT: *"Write a tense standoff between two cowboys who hate each other but keep it civil."* That kind of exchange lets you explore the tension tucked inside polite words, the kind that carry an edge sharper than any blade.

Word choice is another key to nailing that Western voice. Characters didn't talk like professors, and they didn't have to. They used plain words, often colorful, and sometimes invented their own. "He's fixin' to ride out." "That boy's a few beans short of a burrito." "You're playin' with rattlers, son." These expressions give flavor without overdoing it. Ask ChatGPT to help you gather more: *"List authentic 19th-century Western idioms and phrases for everyday situations."* Sprinkle them into dialogue like seasoning—just enough to bring out the taste without overpowering the dish.

Another trick to Western dialogue is to use contradiction and metaphor to show emotion. Folks didn't always say what they meant, especially when it came to fear, grief, or love. "He ain't comin' back" could mean someone's dead, left for good, or just gave up. "Reckon I'll ride a piece with ya" might mean someone's ready to risk their life. Metaphors rooted in the land hit hardest: "Colder than a banker's handshake," or "That man's got a snake where his soul oughta be." These aren't just clever—they're cultural. They speak from the land as much as about it.

You can use ChatGPT to test different characters' voices. Ask it to write the same line from the point of view of a sheriff, an outlaw, a saloon girl, and a preacher. You'll see how voice changes not just with dialect but with status, experience, and attitude. One might be curt. One might be sweet. One might not say much at all. That variation keeps your cast from sounding like a chorus and turns them into a crowd of distinct individuals.

Dialogue in a Western also follows certain rhythms in conflict. In a gunfight, nobody yells out Shakespeare. You get a few quiet words. A threat. A warning. A farewell. "You sure you want to do this?" "Ain't got much choice." "Then let's get to it." Short. Sharp. Taut with finality. ChatGPT can help you write these confrontations. Ask: *"Write a duel scene with sparse, dramatic dialogue between two old enemies."* You'll see how little it takes to make a scene heavy with meaning.

Humor, when it shows up, is dry as a desert bone. Sarcasm is quiet. Jokes are simple but sting. "That horse got more sense than you." "You couldn't pour whiskey from a boot with the instructions on the heel." That kind of talk makes characters feel lived-in, like they've seen too much and learned to laugh so they don't break. Ask ChatGPT for examples: *"Give me ten Western-style insults or jabs between friends."* You'll find gold in the sass.

Writing romantic dialogue in a Western needs a light hand and a heavy heart. People didn't gush. They hinted. They let their guard slip only in rare moments, and then they usually regretted it. A woman might say, "You keep lookin' at me like that and I'll forget I ain't supposed to care." A man might answer, "I ain't never been good at rememberin' what I'm s'posed to do." Ask ChatGPT: *"Write a Western-style conversation between two people in love who are too stubborn to admit it."* What you get will be full of longing and resistance—the two things frontier love was built on.

And don't underestimate silence. Sometimes, saying nothing says everything. A nod. A glance. A shared moment of stillness. In the West, the land didn't say much either, and folks learned to speak the same way. When you write dialogue, let your characters live in that quiet space between words. Let them speak with their eyes, their hands, their hesitation.

So when you sit down to write Western dialogue, don't aim for folksy charm or endless slang. Aim for honesty. Speak like the land does—slow, rough, plain, and true. Let ChatGPT help you shape the drawl, find the metaphor, and trim the fat. Because Western talk isn't about how much you say. It's about what it costs to say it. And in the West, every word ought to carry weight.

Writing Westerns with Moral Grey Areas

If there's one thing that sets a great Western apart from the rest, it's not just the shootouts or sunsets—it's the murkiness in the middle. Westerns aren't about clean lines between good and evil. They're about what happens in the dust between right and wrong. The sheriff who breaks the law to keep the peace. The outlaw who saves a child. The preacher who drinks too much. The land itself doesn't care about your morals, and neither do most of the people trying to survive on it. That's what makes Westerns so compelling. They live in the grey. And when you write with that in mind—especially with ChatGPT helping you flesh it out—you find yourself telling stories that feel honest, rough-edged, and unforgettable.

Start with the idea that nobody in your story is purely good or purely evil. Every character should have reasons, fears, regrets, and contradictions. Maybe your lawman shoots a suspect in cold blood to avoid a trial he knows the town won't survive. Maybe your outlaw robs a bank to fund a school for orphans. These aren't just twists—they're reflections of a world where survival often outweighs virtue. Ask ChatGPT: *"Give me a morally complex Western character who walks the line between justice and revenge."* What you get won't just be a bio—it'll be a philosophy wrapped in boots and regret.

In Westerns, the setting demands compromise. A man may want to be good, but the frontier doesn't always let him. Water is scarce, tempers are short, and justice is often whatever you can enforce with the barrel of a gun. That environment shapes decisions. Your characters may believe in fairness, but when push comes to shove, they'll steal a horse, lie to a friend, or walk away from someone begging for help. Not because they're bad—but because they're desperate. Ask ChatGPT: *"Describe a scene where a woman must choose between saving her brother or telling the truth."* You'll get a fork in the road—one path legal, one path loyal—and both feel wrong.

Moral grey areas are most powerful when they divide characters. Let your cast disagree on what's right. The rancher might think killing rustlers is justice. The schoolteacher might call it murder. The townsfolk might be too afraid to speak up. That disagreement creates drama without needing a villain. Everyone thinks they're doing the right thing—and maybe they all are. You can ask ChatGPT to develop these conflicts: *"Create a group of characters with conflicting views on how to handle a gang threatening their town."* You'll end up with layered perspectives, not just plot devices.

Dialogue is where moral ambiguity comes to life. Don't have characters explain themselves too cleanly. Let their motives leak out sideways—in anger, guilt, or bitter acceptance. A man might say, "Wasn't my choice," when he means, "I made the only choice I could." A woman might spit, "Better me than her," but carry the weight of that decision for years. Use ChatGPT to explore this kind of nuance: *"Write a short exchange where two old friends debate the morality of a killing."* The story in their silence might be louder than their words.

Grey morality also means no easy resolutions. Maybe your protagonist wins the fight but loses his soul. Maybe he rides away, having done the right thing the wrong way, or the wrong thing for the right reason. That sting, that moral residue, is what gives your story teeth. Ask ChatGPT: *"Describe an ending where the hero saves the town but becomes the villain in the eyes of the people."* You'll see how ambiguity doesn't weaken a story—it strengthens it.

And don't forget how the land plays into these moral struggles. Nature is indifferent. It doesn't reward kindness or punish cruelty. That harsh truth makes characters cling harder to their codes—or abandon them entirely. A dying outlaw might confess his sins not to be forgiven, but just to die honestly. A preacher might bury a killer with the same words he'd use for a child. These juxtapositions ground your story in something deeper than genre. They give it gravity. Ask

ChatGPT: *"Write a burial scene for a morally ambiguous character, spoken by someone who loved and hated him."* That kind of moment sticks with a reader.

Even your antagonists deserve layers. The railroad tycoon destroying family farms might have grown up dirt-poor. The gang leader terrorizing the county might be feeding half the town. The bounty hunter chasing your protagonist might believe he's the only one willing to do what's necessary. Use ChatGPT to build these opposing forces: *"Create a Western villain whose actions are evil but motivated by grief."* You'll end up with someone the reader may not forgive—but might understand.

Moral ambiguity also invites the reader or viewer to question their own values. What would *they* do in that situation? Would they forgive? Steal? Kill to protect someone? The best Westerns don't hand out answers—they hold up a mirror. With ChatGPT, you can test different versions of a scene to explore those questions. Try: *"Write two versions of a scene—one where a character shows mercy and one where they take revenge."* Compare the fallout. Let the consequences echo.

Writing a Western with moral grey areas isn't about being edgy. It's about being honest to the world you're building. Life out there was rarely clean. People bent rules, crossed lines, and paid the price. But in that tension—in that slow unraveling between justice and survival, love and vengeance, law and freedom—you find the heart of your story.

So don't be afraid of the grey. Embrace it. Let your characters wrestle with it. Let your audience sit in it. Use ChatGPT to help explore every angle and contradiction. Because in a Western, the most interesting place to be isn't the right side or the wrong side—it's stuck right in the middle, where the dust won't settle and the truth won't come easy. That's where drama lives. That's where your Western finds its voice.

How to Structure a Western Short Story in One Sitting

Writing a Western short story in one sitting isn't about rushing—it's about clarity. You're not aiming for a sprawling epic, you're aiming for a clean, sharp slice of frontier life that lands like a hammer and leaves dust in the reader's lungs. The Western short story is lean, tense, and filled with mood. It knows what it wants to say, gets there with purpose, and doesn't waste a word. When you structure it right, with focus and fire, you can knock out a complete tale in one sitting—and with ChatGPT riding shotgun, you'll never be alone on the trail.

First, start with your ending. That's your campfire in the distance, the place you're riding toward. Do you want to leave the reader with a gut punch, a quiet sigh, or a sharp twist? Knowing how it ends tells you everything about how to begin. Maybe a man dies for the wrong reason. Maybe a woman walks away with the deed to a ranch and blood on her hands. Maybe the hero loses, but the land stays the same. Ask ChatGPT: *"Give me five powerful Western story endings that leave emotional impact."* Pick the one that speaks loudest and start riding toward it.

Once you have your end, sketch the spine. A Western short story rides on tension. Something needs to go wrong fast and keep tightening. Set your character in motion—give them a goal, a threat, and a reason to move now. You don't need elaborate backstory. One strong image can carry the whole thing. A bounty hunter finds a wanted man already dying of disease. A young boy finds his father's buried gun and decides to become something else. A saloon girl poisons the drink of a killer and waits to see who falls first. These aren't plots—they're sparks. Ask ChatGPT: *"Describe a gripping opening for a Western short story involving betrayal."* You'll get a paragraph that might open a door you didn't even know was there.

Keep your cast small. One or two main characters, a side figure at most. You don't have time to build a town—you've got time to build a moment. The reader should feel like they just walked into the middle of something dangerous, important, and irreversible. If you need help cutting the fat, tell ChatGPT: *"Trim this story idea to fit three characters and one setting."* What comes back will be tight enough to grip, but loose enough to breathe.

Choose your setting wisely. A Western short story lives and dies by atmosphere. A canyon at dusk. A barn during a thunderstorm. A lonely jail cell where the wind sounds like a woman crying. Let the setting reflect the theme. If your story's about revenge, set it in the scorched heat of noon. If it's about regret, give it the hush of dawn. Ask ChatGPT: *"Describe a Western setting that echoes a character's internal conflict."* Let that echo build your tone from the first sentence.

Dialogue should be sharp, sparse, and meaningful. Every line should either move the plot or reveal character. And in a short story, the fewer lines, the better. If a man says, "I ain't sorry," and the woman replies, "I ain't askin'," that's enough to carry two whole histories. Ask ChatGPT to polish or generate: *"Write a terse conversation between two characters who used to love each other and now stand on opposite sides of the law."* You'll get sparks. Cut where needed. Let silence do the rest.

As you write, think in scenes. Scene one: something shifts—a stranger rides in, a letter arrives, a secret's revealed. Scene two: choices get harder. The clock's ticking, the stakes are rising, and the land feels tighter. Scene three: the showdown. This doesn't have to be a shootout—but it does need to be a reckoning. Someone gets what they want or what they deserve. Or both. Ask ChatGPT: *"Outline a three-scene structure for a Western about loyalty and betrayal."* It'll give you the skeleton—you bring the muscle and grit.

When pacing your story, don't linger. This isn't a campfire tale drawn out over hours. It's a match strike—hot, quick, and done before you realize how bright it burned. Focus on what matters. The gun in the drawer. The horse untied. The second glass of whiskey untouched. One detail can carry a scene if it's charged right. You can ask ChatGPT: *"List objects that hold emotional significance in a Western short story."* Pick one, build around it.

Use weather, time of day, and silence to your advantage. A story set during a drought feels different than one set in a blizzard. A noon standoff under a burning sun carries different energy than one at midnight with only lamplight and wind. These choices set your pace and build emotion without extra dialogue. Ask ChatGPT to help shape the world around your moment: *"Write a brief Western scene during a storm that foreshadows violence."* The environment should feel like it's leaning in, listening.

And when you reach the end, don't explain it. Let the reader feel it. Let them sit in the dust and silence after the last word, unsure how to feel. That's the beauty of a Western—it lingers. If you've written it well, they'll carry that story in their bones for a while. Ask ChatGPT to help close with impact: *"Write a Western short story ending where the character wins, but it doesn't feel like victory."*

So sit down with your idea. Fire up ChatGPT. Decide what hurts, what's true, and what needs to be done. Set a man or woman on a trail they can't turn back from, and let the land shape the rest. Write like the sun's going down and there's only time for one more tale before the fire dies.

A Western short story doesn't need to be long—it just needs to leave a mark. One sitting. One shot. That's all you need. Now take aim.

Creating a Novel from a Prompt: ChatGPT in Action

One of the most powerful things about using ChatGPT for writing Westerns is how quickly you can go from spark to structure. A single prompt—if crafted with care—can set the whole machine in motion. You don't need to come in with a full outline or even a detailed idea. All you need is a starting point with weight, mood, and a little mystery. From there, ChatGPT can help you build everything from the protagonist's backstory to the final scene of a full-length novel. The magic is in the process, and it all starts with the prompt.

Let's say your prompt is something simple, like: *"A retired gunslinger is forced to pick up his weapon one last time when an outlaw gang returns to a town he once tried to forget."* That's not a whole story, but it's a seed. And with ChatGPT, that seed can grow roots fast. Ask: *"Expand this prompt into a full novel concept with a beginning, middle, and end."* You'll get a structure: the inciting incident, the midpoint twist, the final confrontation. That's your skeleton, and now you can begin to put flesh on the bones.

Next, dive into character. Who is this gunslinger? What broke him before he left the life behind? Who did he lose? What's pulling him back into the fire? Ask ChatGPT: *"Create a character sketch of a former gunslinger haunted by a past mistake."* You'll get everything from physical description to emotional baggage, and you can start building a voice that feels real, tired, and still dangerous.

Now you need supporting characters. A deputy who idolizes him. A saloon owner who still carries a torch. A teenage kid looking for a father figure and a lesson in vengeance. Ask: *"Give me three supporting characters with unique relationships to the protagonist."* Suddenly, you've got layers—people with their own stakes in the outcome, their own motivations, and their own arcs. These are the threads that will make the story rich.

You can then ask ChatGPT to help you develop your setting. Is this a lawless frontier town near the badlands? A fading gold rush camp trying to find purpose now that the gold is gone? A desert settlement surrounded by canyon passes and bandit trails? Try: *"Describe a Western town isolated in the mountains, recovering from a deadly past."* The details you get will help shape the mood and geography of your novel—and make every scene feel rooted in the dust and distance.

Once you have your setting, structure, and characters, it's time to build your chapters. You can go chapter by chapter, feeding ChatGPT your ideas: *"Write a rough draft of Chapter One, where the gunslinger returns to town after ten years."* What comes back won't be your final draft—but it will be something you can revise, reshape, and expand upon. You can even say: *"Make it slower. Add more mood. Make him observe the changes in the town."* And ChatGPT will adjust.

Dialogue is another area where ChatGPT shines. You can take your rough scene and say: *"Rewrite the conversation between the gunslinger and the saloon owner with more subtext and tension."* The result will usually show restraint, loaded lines, and the kind of grit that Western dialogue demands.

If you hit a wall while writing, ChatGPT is your trail guide. Ask: *"What are three possible directions the story could take after Chapter Five, where the gang ambushes the town?"* You'll get options you hadn't considered—maybe the gunslinger's old partner is riding with the outlaws. Maybe the deputy has been compromised. Maybe the town itself turns on the protagonist. These twists can help you stay ahead of your own story, and every time you get stuck, you can simply ask: *"What happens next?"*

You can also use ChatGPT to layer in themes as you go. Want the story to wrestle with forgiveness? Redemption? The cost of violence? Ask: *"How can I show the theme of redemption through the gunslinger's arc without preaching?"* You'll get ideas for small moments—acts of kindness, hesitation before pulling the trigger, a quiet apology in a graveyard. That's the emotional spine that will give your novel weight.

And don't forget pacing. You can step back from the chapters and ask ChatGPT: *"Summarize the story so far and suggest a rising action that builds to the climax."* This helps you keep your story moving with rhythm and momentum, making sure each scene adds pressure instead of just adding pages.

Once you near the end, you can also use prompts to craft a satisfying finish. Maybe the final standoff isn't just about bullets—it's about a choice. Ask: *"Write three alternate endings for a Western where the hero defeats the gang but is offered a chance to take their place."* That kind of dilemma gives your ending complexity, and you can choose the one that hits hardest.

Then, for revisions, you can ask: *"Improve this scene by adding sensory detail and making the tone more reflective."* ChatGPT will give you a polished paragraph that you can mold into your own voice. The idea is not to let AI write the novel for you—it's to let it carry some of the weight, so you can focus on the story you want to tell.

The beauty of using ChatGPT to create a Western novel from a single prompt is that nothing has to be perfect on the first go. You can try, refine, change direction, explore alternatives—all in real time. And in one long, focused session, you could outline an entire book, write three chapters, explore the ending, and shape a cast that feels like they belong in that world of grit, gunpowder, and moral ambiguity.

So start with a sentence. Feed the fire with a question. Let the West unfold before you with every response. Because in the hands of a writer with vision and the right prompts, ChatGPT isn't just a tool—it's the trail horse that'll get you across the badlands of your imagination and straight into the heart of your novel.

Writing a Screenplay in a Day with AI

The idea of writing an entire screenplay in a single day might sound wild—impossible, even—but with the right focus, a clear goal, and a powerful AI like ChatGPT riding shotgun, it's not only doable, it can actually be fun. A screenplay isn't about fancy prose or endless description—it's about structure, intention, visual storytelling, and getting to the heart of the action fast. Western drama, with its lean dialogue, stark environments, and high-stakes conflicts, is the perfect genre for this kind of focused, fast writing sprint. And when you work with ChatGPT as your collaborator, it's like having a writing partner who never gets tired, never runs out of ideas, and always has your back when you hit a wall.

You start with the idea, just a single sentence. That's your campfire spark. Something like: *"A retired bounty hunter must return to the job when his estranged daughter is kidnapped by the son of a man he once gunned down."* Simple, sharp, and packed with potential. That's all you need to start. Feed it to ChatGPT and say: *"Expand this into a one-sentence logline and then a three-act structure for a 90-minute film."* Within seconds, you've got the backbone of your screenplay: your beginning, your midpoint, your climax.

From there, it's about filling in the beats. A solid Western screenplay will usually follow the classic three-act structure, with clear turning points. ChatGPT can lay these out for you: *"Break down this Western into 15 story beats using Save the Cat structure."* You'll get your opening image, your inciting incident, your midpoint reversal, your dark night of the soul—all tailored to the story you gave it.

Once the beats are in place, it's time to build the scenes. Ask: *"Write a screenplay scene where the bounty hunter returns to a ghost town and finds a clue left behind by his daughter."* What you get is formatted in screenplay style, visual, minimal, and ready to drop into your draft. Then you simply build scene after scene, using prompts to guide the story: *"Next, write a scene where he confronts an old rival in a saloon filled with strangers."* And just like that, the story keeps unfolding.

Dialogue becomes its own art form here, and Westerns live or die by their dialogue. You want it lean, loaded with subtext, and tinged with the rhythm of the frontier. ChatGPT is a natural at this. Try: *"Write tense dialogue between the bounty hunter and the villain's henchman, who used to ride together years ago."* You'll get something that hints at history, old wounds, and hidden threats—all within a handful of lines.

And because this is a screenplay, every word counts. Screenwriting isn't about telling—it's about showing. You can tell ChatGPT: *"Rewrite this scene to remove all internal thoughts and focus only on actions and dialogue."* You'll get a tighter version that works on the screen, not just the page. That's key to finishing your script fast: keeping the momentum visual and active.

You can also use AI to generate location ideas quickly. Ask: *"Give me five dramatic Western locations for major scenes in a screenplay."* You'll get atmospheric backdrops like an abandoned mine, a flooded river crossing, a windswept mesa, or a shattered church at the edge of nowhere. These settings don't just look good on screen—they carry story weight and emotional resonance.

When it comes time to shape your character arcs, you can ask: *"Track the emotional arc of the bounty hunter over the course of this screenplay."* ChatGPT can help you show how the character begins as a broken man, becomes a reluctant hero, faces his worst self at the midpoint, and finally redeems himself in the climax—not through speeches, but through action and sacrifice.

If you're running out of steam or hit a dead spot in your writing sprint, just stop and type: *"What happens next?"* The AI will offer a few directions, and even if you don't use them all, they'll help you stay in motion. That's the trick to writing fast—you don't need every scene to be perfect right away. You just need to keep the horse moving forward.

Structure your time like this: an hour for the outline, three hours for the first act, three more for the second, and two for the third. Use ChatGPT to generate, refine, and rearrange as you go. Need to create a montage of the hero preparing for the final fight? Just ask: *"Write a montage scene of a gunslinger gearing up for a final standoff."* You'll get cinematic, beat-by-beat visuals you can drop right into your script.

And when the climax arrives, aim for maximum payoff. Ask ChatGPT: *"Write the final showdown between the bounty hunter and the villain, with callbacks to their shared past."* You'll get a scene loaded with tension, emotion, and resolution. That's how you land the punch. That's how you make your one-day screenplay feel like it took months to craft.

You can even ask ChatGPT to format the entire screenplay using correct script formatting. While it may not be perfect Final Draft standards, it's clean enough to revise and polish later. Just say: *"Format this screenplay for export into a screenwriting program."* Then copy, paste, and tweak.

At the end of your writing sprint, you'll have a full draft. It won't be perfect—but it'll be real, it'll be done, and it'll be something you can work with. That's more than most people get in months. You'll have a complete Western screenplay, driven by your creativity and shaped with the help of a powerful co-writer that doesn't need coffee or sleep.

So don't overthink it. Pick a prompt, load your saddlebag with structure, and start writing. Let ChatGPT help you steer, refine, and fire when it counts. Because out here in the wild country of storytelling, all you need is a spark, a little grit, and the will to see it through. And with AI by your side, writing a screenplay in a day doesn't just become possible—it becomes your new secret weapon.

The Classic Showdown: Tension, Timing, and Pacing

There's nothing more iconic in a Western than the showdown. It's the heartbeat of the genre, the moment everything builds toward, when words fail and only action remains. Whether it's a dusty street at high noon, a saloon floor cleared for space, or a candlelit barn where the past finally catches up, the showdown is more than just a gunfight. It's a reckoning. And the key to writing a great showdown—especially with the help of ChatGPT—isn't just in the shooting, but in the silence before it. Tension, timing, and pacing are what turn a simple exchange of bullets into something unforgettable.

First, let's be clear: a showdown is about more than who draws first. It's about *why* they draw, *when* they draw, and *what's at stake* when the dust settles. Every Western showdown works best when it's loaded with emotional history. These two people didn't just meet five minutes ago—they've been circling each other for miles, years, lifetimes. The bullets are just punctuation marks at the end of a long, slow-burning sentence. You can start building that weight by asking ChatGPT: *"Write a confrontation between a former lawman and the outlaw who killed his brother ten years ago."* What comes back won't be just gunfire—it'll be tension born from grief, regret, and rage.

Now let's talk timing. A great showdown doesn't rush. It stretches. Time slows. You're watching fingers twitch, eyes narrow, breath held. That's what makes the scene feel dangerous. You don't need a lot of words—just the right ones. Maybe one last warning. Maybe a line that stings like a rattler's bite. You can ask ChatGPT: *"Give me ten lines of dialogue that could be spoken just before a Western showdown."* Pick one that makes your skin crawl. That's the one that tells the reader or viewer: this is it.

Pacing is everything here. The moments leading up to the draw should move like a heartbeat in the ear—steady but rising. Use sensory details. The sound of spurs on wood. A breeze that lifts the corner of someone's coat. The slow, deliberate motion of someone wiping dust from their revolver. Ask ChatGPT: *"Describe the thirty seconds before two gunmen draw in a tense Western standoff."* You'll get more than visuals—you'll get atmosphere thick enough to choke on.

You can also build tension by limiting the scene. The fewer people in it, the tighter it feels. If it's a crowd watching from behind windows, have them go silent. If it's two people alone in the desert, let the wind speak. One character might blink more than usual. The other never takes their eyes off the other's hands. These micro-details are where the real pacing lives. The showdown doesn't explode—it coils. Ask ChatGPT: *"Write a paragraph where two characters face off, and nothing happens yet—but it feels like everything will."* That's the pressure you want your audience to feel in their chest.

Once the guns come out, the moment should be quick. Blink-and-you-miss-it quick. Western showdowns don't need long shootouts—they need sharpness. One shot, two at most. It's over as fast as it began, but the aftermath lingers. Someone drops. Someone walks away. Maybe neither does. Ask ChatGPT: *"Write the climax of a Western showdown with minimal action and maximum emotion."* Let the shooting be a whisper. The power comes from what came before—and what follows after.

And what follows matters. The aftermath is part of the pacing, too. Don't just end with a body in the dust. Give us the silence after. The people stepping slowly into the street. The sound of boots walking away. Maybe someone drops the gun they didn't fire. Maybe the survivor doesn't look back. Ask ChatGPT to help you craft this: *"Describe the moments after a Western duel, focusing on emotion and setting."* That's where your story finishes its breath.

Not every showdown has to be between enemies. Sometimes it's between friends who've grown apart. Sometimes it's between two people who don't hate each other—but can't back down. Sometimes it's even internal—a character staring at themselves in a mirror, gun in hand, unsure if they're the villain now. Ask ChatGPT: *"Write a non-violent Western showdown between two people who used to love each other."* You'll find the same tension, just fired in words instead of bullets.

You can also use environment to shape your showdown. A blizzard makes every movement difficult. A cliffside makes every step dangerous. A crowded saloon turns witnesses into pressure points. Each setting changes the pace, because each place carries different risks. Ask ChatGPT: *"Describe a Western showdown in a thunderstorm, with limited visibility."* That tension doesn't just come from the guns—it comes from the world holding its breath.

And remember, not every showdown needs to end with death. Sometimes the gun stays holstered. Sometimes one person walks away, because killing them wouldn't fix anything. That restraint can be more powerful than any bullet. ChatGPT can help you explore that too: *"Write a Western standoff where the protagonist chooses not to shoot."* Let the reader feel the weight of that choice—and what it costs.

So when you're writing a showdown, slow down. Let the moment stretch like leather pulled tight. Let the silence talk. Let the hands hover. Let the stakes bleed into every glance and breath. Use ChatGPT to sculpt the language, tweak the timing, and test the scene until it feels like a storm ready to break.

Because the classic Western showdown isn't just about who's faster on the draw—it's about what it means when someone finally does.

Themes of Freedom and Fate in the Wild West

If there are two ideas that sit at the heart of every great Western, it's freedom and fate. They're tangled like barbed wire and dry brush, pulling at each other in every scene, in every decision, in every ride into the unknown. Out West, freedom is the dream. Fate is the shadow. Together, they create the tension that drives Western drama, giving it more than grit and guns—they give it soul.

Freedom in the West isn't some abstract ideal. It's the reason people leave everything behind, why they build towns in deserts, why they live off the land instead of within the laws. A cowboy rides not because he's going somewhere, but because he can. A woman runs a boarding house on her own terms because she won't be owned by any man or system. A former outlaw hides in plain sight, choosing peace over pursuit. These stories revolve around the idea that out here, a person can reinvent themselves, break their past, rewrite their future. Freedom is the promise carved into the horizon line.

You can explore this by asking ChatGPT: *"Describe a Western protagonist who is chasing personal freedom in a land full of old debts."* You'll get a character who isn't just moving forward—they're running from chains that aren't always physical. That's where the real drama comes from. Because freedom, in Westerns, always costs something. Comfort. Safety. Connection. And sometimes, even the dream of it turns out to be a mirage.

Fate, meanwhile, rides just behind. You might run, but it's always close. In the West, fate feels carved into the dust. Maybe it's a prophecy, or a name whispered in fear, or a choice made long ago that just won't die. A man might try to live clean, but the blood on his hands won't wash off. A woman might marry into a quiet life, but the ghosts of her past come knocking when the sun goes down. Fate in a Western isn't just about what happens—it's about what *has to happen*.

Try a prompt like: *"Write a scene where a gunslinger faces the man he's been trying to avoid for ten years."* That's fate knocking. He knew it would come. He just hoped it wouldn't be today. The tension in that moment—the weight of inevitability—is what separates a Western from just another action tale. It's not just about survival. It's about the feeling that no matter how far you ride, the end is riding too.

And sometimes, fate and freedom meet head-on. That's when a character gets to choose whether they're ruled by their past or by what they're willing to do now. That moment of choice is gold for Western drama. A man might stand on a cliff's edge, the law closing in, and decide whether to fight or fall. A woman might be offered a new life but has to betray someone to take it. Ask ChatGPT: *"Give me a character torn between a chance at freedom and loyalty to someone they love."* That's not just plot. That's the West, in its rawest form—freedom laced with consequences, fate twisted in the details.

The land itself becomes a metaphor for both. Vast, open spaces symbolize freedom—limitless, untamed, and full of possibility. But that same openness can feel like a trap when there's nowhere to hide. The desert doesn't care about your intentions. The mountains don't bend to your dreams. The West is beautiful, but indifferent. It gives and it takes. You can use ChatGPT to shape this tone: *"Describe a Western setting that represents both hope and doom."* These are places where freedom whispers and fate waits.

These themes also work powerfully in character relationships. One person might believe in making their own destiny. Another might believe in luck, fate, or God's plan. Put them in a situation where only one of them can be right. Maybe a bounty hunter believes people can change. Maybe his partner believes people *don't*. Maybe they're both wrong. Ask

ChatGPT: *"Create a dialogue between two characters debating whether fate or free will controls their lives."* The tension doesn't need bullets—it comes from beliefs clashing like thunder.

Western stories often end with a strange mix of both themes. The hero dies, but on their own terms. The town is saved, but the cost is high. The outlaw rides into the sunset, not free from the law, but free from his past. These endings don't fit into neat boxes—they linger. They ask questions. Was it worth it? Was this the only way it could have gone? You can ask ChatGPT: *"Write a Western story ending that explores both the cost of freedom and the power of fate."* The result will likely feel both final and haunting.

Freedom and fate also echo through symbolism. The trail represents choice. The gun represents control—or the loss of it. A broken spur, a sunset, a pocket watch stopped at a specific time—all these become totems that carry weight. Use them in your story not just as decoration but as quiet reminders of what your characters believe about their future. Ask ChatGPT: *"Give me five symbolic objects in a Western that represent freedom or fate."* Use those symbols to say what your characters can't.

At the heart of it, Westerns remind us that freedom is never free, and fate is never simple. The tension between the two is what makes your story live and breathe. Every ride into town, every whispered prayer, every finger hovering over a trigger is a step on a path that might be chosen—or might be destined.

When you build your Western world with these themes in mind, you give it depth. You give your characters stakes that go beyond the plot. You give your readers and viewers something to feel long after the dust settles.

So whether you're writing with AI or staring down the blank page on your own, keep those two words in your saddlebag—freedom and fate. Let them shape your story's tone, your character's choices, your ending's weight. Because in the West, those two forces ride together. And between them, legends are born.

Writing from the Outlaw's Perspective

There's a reason the outlaw has always been one of the most compelling figures in Western storytelling. He rides alone, answers to no one, lives by a code of his own making, and carries the weight of the choices that set him apart from the rest of the world. Writing from the outlaw's perspective gives you access to a voice that's raw, unpredictable, and often more honest than the lawmen chasing him. The outlaw sees the world from the edges—unfiltered by law or expectation—and when you sit inside his mind, the Western becomes something more than cowboys and shootouts. It becomes a study in survival, consequence, and the cost of freedom.

To write a believable outlaw, you have to first understand what made him. Nobody just wakes up and decides to rob a bank, rustle cattle, or live with a price on their head. There's a wound behind every wanted poster. Maybe it's a betrayal. Maybe it's poverty. Maybe it's vengeance, pride, or desperation. Ask ChatGPT: *"Create a backstory for a Western outlaw who never intended to become a criminal."* You'll get a layered character who didn't start bad—he just ran out of good options. And that's what makes the outlaw sympathetic even when he's doing something wrong.

Writing in the outlaw's voice means tapping into that mix of defiance and regret. He might not apologize for what he's done, but he remembers it. He might say he doesn't care, but he sleeps with one eye open and doesn't keep friends for long. When you ask ChatGPT to write journal entries, monologues, or inner thoughts from an outlaw's point of view, focus on contradiction. Try a prompt like: *"Write an internal monologue from a Western outlaw waiting for sunrise before a duel."* What you'll get is tension wrapped in guilt, pride, fear, and maybe even hope—because even outlaws hope, they just don't show it.

Another important part of writing from the outlaw's perspective is understanding how he sees the law—and those who enforce it. To him, the sheriff is just another kind of killer, but with a badge and a cleaner conscience. The townsfolk are hypocrites—afraid of men like him but eager to cheer when someone else pulls the trigger. This viewpoint isn't necessarily wrong—it's just skewed by experience. You can explore this with ChatGPT by asking: *"Describe how a Western outlaw might see the justice system of a frontier town."* That response will help you write a narrator or protagonist who's jaded, sharp, and never quite trusts anyone who doesn't have scars of their own.

The outlaw's relationships are often tense, transactional, or fleeting. He might love, but he won't settle. He might ride with others, but trust is always on a thread. The closer someone gets, the more dangerous it feels—for both of them. Ask ChatGPT: *"Write a scene between a Western outlaw and the woman who wants to run away with him."* The emotional core of that interaction will tell you everything about who this man is, and what he's afraid to want.

When you write action from the outlaw's point of view, make it instinctual. He doesn't think through every step—he reacts. Years of life outside the law have taught him to move fast, trust his gut, and never hesitate. When you use ChatGPT to write a gunfight or a chase from this perspective, ask for sensory detail: *"Write a Western action scene from the POV of an outlaw escaping through a canyon."* What comes back should feel like adrenaline—sharp, dirty, desperate, and alive.

But don't forget the quiet moments. The outlaw doesn't just ride and shoot—he waits, watches, remembers. Maybe he sits by a campfire staring at a wanted poster with his own face on it. Maybe he reads an old letter he never sent. These quiet scenes are where the humanity slips through. They show the man behind the myth. Ask ChatGPT: *"Write a reflective scene where a Western outlaw considers turning himself in."* The story in that scene might say more than ten pages of action ever could.

Also consider how the world treats him. Is he famous, infamous, or just another man with blood on his boots? Maybe children play games pretending to be him. Maybe saloons whisper his name like a ghost story. Or maybe he's one of a hundred forgotten riders who'll end up buried in a nameless grave. This larger reputation adds weight to his every step. You can use ChatGPT to explore this myth-making: *"Describe how the legend of a notorious outlaw spreads through the frontier."* Then decide how much of that legend he actually believes.

Writing from the outlaw's perspective also gives you the chance to flip Western conventions. Maybe your outlaw doesn't believe in violence. Maybe he only robs from those who profit off others' misery. Maybe he's been framed and keeps running not because he's guilty, but because he knows no one will believe the truth. These angles breathe fresh life into old tropes. Ask ChatGPT: *"Create a morally complex Western outlaw with a secret that would clear his name."* What you get might turn into a whole novel or screenplay.

And when it comes time to end your story, don't feel like you have to redeem him. Sometimes, the outlaw doesn't get a happy ending. He dies in the dirt, nameless and alone. Sometimes he vanishes into the desert, never to be seen again. And sometimes—just sometimes—he gets to ride away free, scarred but breathing, a legend with dust on his boots. You can ask ChatGPT to explore all three: *"Write three possible endings for a Western outlaw story: tragic, redemptive, and ambiguous."*

Writing from the outlaw's perspective is about more than just turning the tables—it's about writing from the edge. From the place where rules blur, where survival costs something, and where a man's worth is measured not by how clean his hands are, but by how long he can ride with his head held high. Use ChatGPT to dig into the dirt, to find the voice that sounds like whiskey and regret, and to tell the story of someone who doesn't ask to be forgiven—just remembered.

Because when you write from the outlaw's side of the saddle, you don't just get a new angle. You get to write the West with its mask off. And sometimes, that's where the truth really lives.

Crafting the Lawman's Inner Struggles

The Western lawman isn't just a man with a badge—he's a man walking a razor-thin line between justice and vengeance, between order and chaos, between who he was and who he needs to be to keep the peace. He might be sheriff, marshal, or deputy, but his authority often ends where the town border meets the wilderness. And what makes him compelling isn't the size of his gun or the weight of his reputation—it's the storm brewing behind his eyes. Writing the lawman's inner struggle means digging past the badge to find the man underneath, and letting the story show the toll justice takes on a soul.

Western lawmen live in a world where rules are written in dust and blood. They try to hold the line in towns too wild to tame, where the law is often whatever can be enforced by a man standing alone. That's a heavy burden, especially when that lawman knows he's not always right. Maybe he's done things he regrets. Maybe he's bent the rules to protect people. Maybe he's killed when he didn't have to. Ask ChatGPT: *"Create a Western sheriff who is haunted by a past mistake that no one else knows about."* What you get is the emotional skeleton of a great character—someone trying to do the right thing while dragging chains behind him.

That's where the real story lives. Not in the shootouts, but in the quiet decisions. The lawman who lets a desperate thief go free. The one who locks up a friend. The one who stares at his badge and wonders if he deserves to wear it anymore. These are the choices that define him—and that torment him. Try a prompt like: *"Write a scene where a marshal must choose between upholding the law or protecting a loved one."* You'll feel the tension pull tight across the scene like stretched wire.

The lawman's inner world is also shaped by isolation. He's trusted by few, feared by some, and often resented by many. When he walks into a saloon, conversation stops. When he rides out alone, he knows no one's got his back. That solitude breeds reflection, and sometimes doubt. You can ask ChatGPT: *"Write a monologue from a Western lawman who feels he's becoming the very thing he's supposed to stop."* That kind of voice gives your character depth that sticks with the reader long after the story's done.

He may carry the title of sheriff, but inside, he's a man grappling with what that role means when the world doesn't play fair. Maybe the law says one thing, but his gut says another. Maybe the town wants blood, but he's the only one willing to say no. Or maybe he's just tired—of the killing, the compromise, the weight of being everyone's last resort. Ask ChatGPT: *"Describe the emotional toll on a small-town sheriff who hasn't had a day of peace in five years."* That emotional fatigue can shape everything—from how he talks to his deputy to how long he pauses before drawing his weapon.

The lawman's relationships also reveal his cracks. Maybe he drinks too much because it helps him sleep. Maybe his marriage is held together with silence. Maybe his oldest friend is now the town drunk he once jailed. These aren't just side plots—they're pressure points. Every good Western lawman has someone or something he's trying to protect, and when that thing is threatened, the weight of his duty gets heavier. Ask ChatGPT: *"Write a conversation between a sheriff and his estranged wife, where the law has come between them."* That's the kind of personal conflict that makes a gunfight feel earned.

He also sees things others don't. He sees the bodies no one claims. The kids left behind. The way a man changes when he's about to lie. This gives him wisdom—but it also gives him scars. Every decision leaves a mark. Every time he draws blood, he hears the echo later. He may stand tall in the daylight, but it's the night-time when the ghosts come knocking.

Ask: *"Describe a Western sheriff's recurring nightmare that reflects his guilt."* You'll find symbols, moments, and memories that can appear again and again in your story—reminders that the job never really leaves him.

Writing from the lawman's perspective is also a chance to explore justice not as a concept, but as a burden. What happens when he has to enforce a law he doesn't agree with? What does he do when the outlaw is someone he used to ride with? Or when the real villain wears a suit and funds the town's development? The lawman doesn't have the luxury of clean choices. He has to act, often fast, and live with the fallout. You can use ChatGPT to explore this ambiguity: *"Write a scene where a lawman lets a criminal go, knowing it may cost him his badge."* That kind of inner battle builds the kind of tension that doesn't fade with the gun smoke.

And maybe he's nearing the end. Maybe this is his last year with a badge, and he knows the West is changing. Railroads are coming. Banks are replacing saloons. Maybe he doesn't belong anymore. That disillusionment—the slow understanding that his kind is fading—is one of the most poignant themes in Westerns. Ask ChatGPT: *"Write a reflective scene of a sheriff looking out over his town, knowing it doesn't need him much longer."* That's not a plot point—it's the soul of your story.

So when you write the lawman, don't make him invincible. Don't make him perfect. Make him human. Give him doubts, flaws, fears, and regrets. Let him lose control. Let him fight not just against outlaws, but against the part of himself that's been twisted by the job. And use ChatGPT to help shape that inner landscape—through dialogue, dreams, memories, and hard choices.

Because the lawman doesn't wear the badge to feel powerful. He wears it because someone has to. And the longer he wears it, the more it weighs. That weight—that quiet struggle between justice and self—is where the Western gets its heart. That's where the story breathes. And that's where your lawman becomes unforgettable.

Writing the Native American Character with Respect

One of the most important responsibilities a writer takes on when working in the Western genre is how they choose to represent Native American characters. For too long, these characters were sidelined, stereotyped, or reduced to tropes—portrayed either as villains or mystics, rarely as full human beings with depth, agency, and voice. If you're going to include Native American characters in your Western story, especially with the power of ChatGPT helping to build your world, the goal should be authenticity, dignity, and respect. That means doing your homework, slowing down, and listening to the people whose ancestors lived these stories, not just retelling history from the perspective of those who wrote it with ink dipped in conquest.

Writing Native characters with respect begins with understanding they are not monoliths. There were and are hundreds of distinct nations, each with its own language, traditions, social structures, beliefs, and ways of life. The Lakota are not the Navajo. The Apache are not the Cheyenne. Their histories, their lands, and their responses to colonization were different. When you decide to include a Native character, start by asking: *Which nation is this person from? What time period am I writing in, and where are they geographically?* You can prompt ChatGPT with: *"Tell me about the culture, customs, and historical context of the Nez Perce tribe in the 1870s."* This gives you grounding, not just decoration—context that informs your character's worldview, behavior, and values.

Avoid turning Native characters into metaphors or plot devices for the white protagonist's growth. They're not here to teach, rescue, or die for someone else's redemption. They have their own stories, shaped by their own people, and those stories deserve the same emotional space and complexity you would give to any main character. Ask ChatGPT: *"Create a fully developed Native American protagonist from the Lakota nation during the post-Civil War era."* Focus on their internal struggles, hopes, and conflicts. Let them be brave, scared, flawed, wise, foolish—everything that makes a character real.

Language is powerful. Using slurs, even if "historically accurate," can do more harm than good unless handled with extreme care and context. If you're writing a racist character in a historical setting, be mindful of the balance between reflecting the reality of prejudice and reinforcing harmful ideas. Let ChatGPT help you handle it carefully: *"Write a scene that addresses historical racism against Native Americans without glorifying or centering it."* You can present injustice while still making it clear where the moral center of your story lies.

Stereotypes to avoid include the "noble savage," the "wise elder," the "savage warrior," and the "vanishing Indian." These reduce characters to fixed roles instead of people. A Native American doesn't have to be spiritual to be valid, doesn't have to be a warrior to be strong, doesn't have to be in conflict with the settler to be relevant. Instead, write individuals. A young woman trying to learn both her people's traditions and how to speak English. An elder who mistrusts all outsiders but secretly tends to an injured settler. A father who agrees to guide a wagon train, not because he believes in the journey, but because he's looking for something he lost. Ask ChatGPT: *"Describe a Native American character navigating both cultural preservation and frontier encroachment."* This helps you avoid clichés and write someone with depth and realism.

Also consider how your Native characters interact with the land. Their connection to nature isn't mystical—it's practical, sacred, lived. They don't need to recite poetry about buffalo or whisper to the wind unless it fits their specific tradition and character. The land provided food, medicine, shelter, and spiritual meaning—and it was stolen, desecrated, fenced off. Writing a Native character's relationship with the land can be powerful when it reflects loss, protection, or deep generational memory. Ask ChatGPT: *"Write a scene where a Native elder teaches a child about their ancestral land while knowing it may be lost."* That's not mysticism—that's truth.

Dialogue also matters. A Native American character should speak like a person shaped by their culture and era—not like a caricature. Don't default to broken English or mystical metaphors unless you've researched whether that speech pattern is appropriate for their nation and context. Many tribes had multilingual members, especially in later years. Some spoke perfect English, others didn't. Respect the nuance. Ask ChatGPT: *"Help write realistic, respectful dialogue for a Native American woman speaking to a settler in 1880s Arizona."* Let tone, purpose, and history guide the words—not stereotype.

One way to write respectfully is to give your Native characters real agency. They make choices. They disagree with each other. They love, laugh, protect, and mourn. They're not just reacting to what the white characters are doing—they're driving their own lives. Maybe a tribal leader chooses not to fight because he's seen too much death. Maybe a young warrior breaks tribal rules to defend a settler woman who showed him kindness. Maybe a woman flees the reservation not to assimilate—but to find freedom on her own terms. Ask ChatGPT: *"Write a plot where a Native American character is the moral center of the story."* That will show you just how powerful these characters can be when written with depth.

If your story includes historical violence—massacres, forced removals, broken treaties—don't look away from it. But don't make it trauma porn, either. These events were real, and they devastated generations, but they're not the only thing Native characters are built from. Strength, resistance, family, ceremony, and humor are just as vital. You can use ChatGPT to explore this balance: *"Write a scene of resilience within a Native community after a violent loss."* That scene might be quiet—a meal shared, a story told, a song sung—but it's powerful.

Above all, humility is key. If you're not from a Native background, you're entering someone else's story space. That means research, consultation, and sensitivity. Use ChatGPT to gather information, yes—but don't stop there. Read books by Native authors. Watch films by Native filmmakers. Listen to contemporary Native voices. They'll tell you what Westerns got wrong—and what you can do better.

Because writing Native American characters in a Western isn't about adding authenticity—it's about restoring truth. It's about giving voice to the people who were always there, whose stories didn't begin with the arrival of settlers and don't end when the credits roll. When written with care, respect, and curiosity, your story doesn't just become stronger—it becomes more human. And that's what the Western always needs more of.

Guns and Justice: Creating the Myth of the West

The American West, as we often imagine it, never truly existed in the way movies and dime novels told it. But that's exactly what makes it such fertile ground for storytelling. The West, as a myth, was built from grit, gunfire, dusty ideals, and the endless struggle between chaos and law. It's a place where justice rides on horseback and where one man, armed with nothing but a gun and a personal code, could stand against the world. To write Western drama that captures this mythos, especially with ChatGPT as your creative ally, is to step into a space where fact and fiction blend into something far more enduring—legend.

At the heart of the myth is the gun. In Western storytelling, a revolver isn't just a weapon—it's a symbol. It represents freedom, power, fear, control, and justice, often all at once. The gun gives agency to characters who have little else. A poor rancher with a six-shooter can protect what's his. A lone drifter with a rifle can level the playing field against a town full of corruption. But guns also complicate everything. They blur the lines between right and wrong, especially when they become the only way to settle disputes. Ask ChatGPT: *"Describe how a Western protagonist views his gun—as tool, symbol, or burden."* The answer you get could define your entire character's arc.

And then there's justice—that elusive, often twisted ideal that drives most Western plots. Out West, the law is rarely clean. The sheriff might be as crooked as the outlaw. The judge might have a price. The town might cheer a hanging, right or wrong. But justice, in the myth of the West, isn't found in courthouses—it's found in personal codes. Each character defines justice in their own way. One believes in retribution, another in redemption. One might die to uphold it, another might kill to avenge it. You can explore this with ChatGPT: *"Create a conflict between two characters who both believe they are seeking justice, but their methods clash."* That tension creates some of the richest storytelling in the genre.

Guns and justice become inseparable in the Western myth because violence is often the only means by which justice can be delivered. But here's where it gets interesting: most of the best Westerns are about the *consequences* of that violence. The gun solves problems—but it creates others. A man who kills to defend his family may find himself hunted, isolated, changed. A sheriff who shoots an outlaw in the name of justice might lose the respect of the town—or himself. You can dig into this with a prompt like: *"Write a scene where a character questions whether killing in the name of justice was truly justified."* This moral ambiguity is the gold vein in Western drama.

The myth of the West also relies heavily on imagery. A lone rider on the horizon. A pistol on a worn leather belt. A lawman standing between a mob and a cell. These are the visual shorthand of justice and gunsmithing—symbols that immediately evoke the struggle between order and chaos. Ask ChatGPT: *"Describe a cinematic Western scene that visually contrasts justice and lawlessness."* Use that response to set tone, atmosphere, and meaning without needing a single line of dialogue.

One of the reasons guns and justice feel so intertwined in Westerns is because so many characters in this world are seeking redemption or revenge—or both. A man with blood on his hands trying to make peace with his past. A woman whose family was taken, now seeking her own justice. These characters don't wait for the law to catch up—they *are* the law, in their own eyes. And that self-appointed authority is both dangerous and deeply compelling. You can ask ChatGPT to explore this: *"Create a character who sees themselves as a necessary outlaw in pursuit of justice."* The result might blur your audience's moral compass—and that's the whole point.

There's also the myth of the duel—the idea that justice is best served face to face, with no crowd, no law, no jury. Just two people, one truth, and six bullets. This idea has fueled generations of stories because it strips justice down to its barest bones: courage, skill, and resolve. But even this romanticized moment carries layers. Maybe one of them doesn't want to shoot. Maybe the other knows he deserves it. Maybe neither of them walks away feeling like they've won anything. Ask ChatGPT: *"Write a Western duel scene where both participants question the justice of what they're doing."* The emotional charge in that scene can carry your entire story.

Of course, no myth lives without a lie. The myth of the West often erases the truth of who lived there, who suffered, and who was written out of the narrative. Native peoples, Black settlers, Chinese railroad workers, Mexican families—many contributed to the West, and many were victims of the same gun-and-justice philosophy that the myth romanticizes. When writing your story, don't shy away from this. Instead, use it to add depth. You can explore the contrast between the myth and the reality with prompts like: *"Describe a character disillusioned with the idea of frontier justice."* Their perspective can provide a necessary counterweight to the larger-than-life ideals.

Even the gun itself can be a symbol of transformation. A character might bury it, refuse to use it, or break it apart—only to find it again when forced to confront what they thought they'd left behind. In Western storytelling, that choice says everything. Ask ChatGPT: *"Write a scene where a character decides whether to pick up their gun one last time."* That moment becomes not just about survival, but identity.

When you put it all together—the gun, the badge, the code, the silence, the showdown—you're not just writing action. You're writing myth. A story that speaks to something older than the West itself. A story about power and limits, justice and the price of peace. Use ChatGPT to test ideas, draft scenes, and explore alternatives, but always remember: the myth of the West isn't in what actually happened—it's in what we *believe* happened, what we *need* to believe.

Because out there in the dust, where the law's written in blood and carried on the wind, guns and justice aren't just tools or themes. They're the bones of the story. And it's your job, as the writer, to give them flesh—and meaning.

Saloons and Brothels: Writing Life on the Edge

If the sheriff's office was the face of order in the Old West, then the saloon and the brothel were its wild, beating heart. These places weren't just dens of sin or stages for brawls and piano tunes—they were where the real stories unfolded. Life in the saloon was always on the edge of something: violence, lust, regret, confession, deals made in whispers, and lives changed in the time it took to pour a drink. Writing these spaces with authenticity and emotional weight brings your Western drama to life, and with the help of ChatGPT, you can go far deeper than swinging doors and barroom clichés.

Start by seeing the saloon not as a set piece, but as a character. It has a mood, a rhythm, and a memory. It might be a muddy, smoke-choked room lit by oil lamps and filled with the stench of sweat, tobacco, and spilled liquor. Or it might be the most sophisticated structure in a frontier town—plush velvet curtains, a poker table backed by a man with a hidden Derringer, and women in corsets with secrets more dangerous than any gun. Ask ChatGPT: *"Describe a saloon that has seen gunfights, weddings, and betrayals—all under the same roof."* That kind of setting isn't just visual—it tells you what's happened and what could happen again.

The brothel, often part of or adjoining the saloon, holds a different kind of tension. It's easy to reduce these characters—usually women—to background noise or tired tropes, but that's a mistake. The women who worked in these places often had more insight into the power dynamics of the town than the lawman or the preacher. They heard the confessions, witnessed the deals, and sometimes even held the strings. Some were victims. Some were survivors. Some were businesswomen sharper than any banker. Ask ChatGPT: *"Create a brothel madam who runs her business with intelligence and hidden influence in a Western town."* What you get will probably carry more narrative weight than half the town's elected officials.

Writing the atmosphere of these places means capturing the edge—the sense that anything can happen at any moment. A man walks in with revenge on his mind. A stranger at the piano plays a song no one's heard in years. A card game turns sour. A woman recognizes a face from a past life she thought she buried. The tension in a saloon or brothel doesn't need to explode—it simmers. Ask ChatGPT: *"Write a scene in a Western saloon where the mood shifts from laughter to deadly quiet."* You'll feel that edge sharpen as the scene unfolds.

Dialogue in these spaces carries extra heat. In a saloon, every word can be a threat, an invitation, or a challenge. In a brothel, words can conceal longing, manipulation, or cold calculation. The characters in these places speak in code, in double meanings, in tone more than text. A barkeep might say, *"He's had enough,"* meaning someone better take his gun before he starts swinging. A woman might say, *"You look like trouble,"* meaning she's seen someone like this before—and it didn't end well. Ask ChatGPT: *"Write a tense conversation between a brothel madam and a drifter she recognizes from ten years ago."* That scene writes itself once the unspoken fills the room.

Use saloons and brothels to introduce story catalysts. Maybe the outlaw the lawman's chasing is hiding out there. Maybe the madam knows the truth about a murder the sheriff can't solve. Maybe the piano player is a fugitive in disguise. These places are where secrets leak and alliances shift. Ask ChatGPT to brainstorm: *"List five story twists that could unfold in a Western saloon."* You'll end up with enough material to spark a full subplot or even the main arc of your story.

These places are also ideal for exploring class, gender, and power in subtle but powerful ways. The wealthy cattleman might think he owns the town until a woman he tried to forget appears in the saloon with a pistol in her purse and truth on her tongue. The saloon girl who's been dismissed as decoration might be spying for someone—or plotting something herself. Ask ChatGPT: *"Write a scene where a saloon girl uses her underestimated status to influence a powerful man."* The moment will do more than surprise—it'll reframe your whole cast.

It's also important to show the daily life in these places—not just the chaos. A tired bartender sweeping up glass. A woman fixing her hair in the mirror while hiding bruises. A young boy delivering supplies, wide-eyed and quiet. These details bring humanity to what could otherwise become set dressing. Ask: *"Describe the morning routine of a brothel after a long night in an 1880s Western town."* You'll get a sense of realism that grounds your world in lived experience.

Don't forget that these places often walked the line between survival and destruction. For some, the saloon or brothel was the only place that offered a meal and a bed. For others, it was a trap. Addiction, violence, and exploitation were common. But so were friendship, loyalty, laughter, and escape. The edge wasn't just danger—it was possibility. A character might find their purpose behind the bar or lose everything in a backroom game. Ask ChatGPT: *"Write a turning point scene that takes place in a Western brothel between two unlikely allies."* That's the kind of moment that reveals who people really are.

And when you write these scenes, don't be afraid of contrast. Let joy exist beside despair. Let music play while blood dries on the floor. Let a joke make someone laugh just before the hammer of a revolver clicks into place. That's what life on the edge feels like—impossibly full and constantly shifting. It's chaotic, messy, and deeply human.

So when you write your saloon or your brothel, don't write scenery. Write life. Let the people who work there, drink there, and haunt those walls breathe. Use ChatGPT to shape their voices, histories, and desires. Let those spaces be crossroads—of passion and regret, of hope and collapse. Because in the West, it wasn't the courthouse or the church where stories were made.

It was the saloon.

It was the brothel.

It was the edge.

Revenge, Redemption, and Everything Between

The Western thrives on big emotions carved into quiet characters. And few themes cut deeper—or ride harder—than revenge and redemption. These are the twin rails your story can travel, bending every decision your characters make, pulling them toward violence, forgiveness, or something messier and more real. In the Western, revenge is rarely clean. Redemption is never easy. And the best stories ride the jagged trail between the two, where justice gets cloudy, blood cries out, and the soul is tested one hard mile at a time.

Revenge is a familiar engine for a Western. Someone's been wronged—by a gang, a rival, a town, or even their own kin—and now the only thing that matters is settling the score. It's primal, understandable, and dangerous. Writing from this place means giving your character a wound that won't close, something raw and burning that shapes every step they take. But here's the key—revenge always changes a person. Sometimes it transforms them. Sometimes it destroys them. Ask ChatGPT: *"Create a Western character driven by revenge, but who begins to question the cost."* The story begins when the vengeance starts to hollow them out.

Revenge makes your protagonist active. They ride into town with purpose. They ask questions with fists. They make enemies fast. But it also blinds them. They start seeing people as obstacles, not humans. That's where your story finds its heart—when someone or something shakes that single-mindedness and forces your character to face the mirror. Maybe it's a child caught in the crossfire. Maybe it's a friend who warns them they're becoming like the one they're chasing. Use a prompt like: *"Write a confrontation between a revenge-driven gunslinger and a childhood friend who tries to stop them."* That's when the real emotional bullets start flying.

On the other side of the dusty coin is redemption. And it never comes easy. No Western hero is born clean. They've done things. Things they don't speak of. Things they think can't be undone. Redemption in the West doesn't come with applause—it comes with blood, with sacrifice, with silence. Writing a character seeking redemption means giving them guilt they wear like a second skin. It could be something they did, something they didn't do, or someone they couldn't save. Ask ChatGPT: *"Describe a Western outlaw trying to make peace with his past through small, unspoken acts."* This is a man or woman who might never be forgiven—but that doesn't mean they stop trying.

Redemption often hides in the small things. Giving a hungry stranger food. Protecting someone they don't owe. Turning themselves in. Or just choosing not to draw when they easily could. It's in restraint, not triumph. And sometimes, they never get there. Sometimes they try and fail. Sometimes redemption isn't granted—but they reach for it anyway. That reach, that effort—that's what moves the reader. Ask: *"Write the final thoughts of a dying character who tried to do one good thing before the end."* It won't need a lot of words. The West doesn't use many. But it'll hit hard.

And then there's the space between. That wide, dusty middle ground where most of your characters actually live. People who want revenge but don't know if they'll go through with it. People who want redemption but don't think they deserve it. People torn between justice and mercy, between blood and forgiveness. That's the richest place to write from. Ask ChatGPT: *"Create a Western plot where the protagonist switches from revenge to redemption halfway through the story."* That moment of change—that hesitation at the edge of the cliff—is where your story finds its soul.

The best Westerns let both themes exist in one character. A former killer who becomes a protector. A lawman who seeks justice but hides his own crimes. A woman who burns down a town for revenge, then rebuilds it from the ashes. Use duality to make your characters real. Give them motives that conflict. Let them doubt. Let them regret. Ask ChatGPT:

"Write an internal monologue of a Western character who has just gotten revenge but feels no peace." That's where the gun's been fired, but the story's not over—because the heart still beats with questions.

Symbolism plays beautifully with these themes. A blood-stained letter. A wedding ring still worn. A shovel used to bury both the past and the future. Redemption and revenge both live in objects, in memories, in rituals. A man might clean his gun every night—not because he's preparing for violence, but because he can't forgive himself for the last time he used it. Ask: *"Give me five symbolic objects that represent guilt and redemption in a Western setting."* They'll give your story texture and weight.

And then there's the question: is redemption possible in a world built on survival? Can someone who's done unspeakable things still do something good? Not perfect. Just good. That's the question every great Western asks. And maybe the answer isn't yes or no—it's: *they tried.* They tried to be better. Even if it was too late. Even if it cost them everything. And that trying? That's the story.

So let your characters ride with fury in their hearts. Let them ache to make it right. Let them fall somewhere between the man who can't forget and the one who's learning how to live with it. Use ChatGPT to shape their journey. Map their inner terrain. Build scenes that test them, tempt them, push them toward the edge and see if they jump—or climb back.

Because in the West, revenge might start the ride.

But it's redemption—or the hope of it—that makes the dust settle just a little quieter in the end.

Survival Stories on the Prairie

The prairie looks endless. Open skies. Grasses that ripple like waves. A wind that never sleeps. It can be beautiful—until you realize just how far away everything is. No help. No shelter. No mercy. Out here, survival is a story all its own. It's not always about shootouts or standoffs. Sometimes it's about enduring. About watching the sky for storms. About digging a well that might not hit water. About hoping your last bullet isn't the one you have to use on yourself. Writing a survival story on the prairie is about stripping life to its bones and finding what's left when everything else is gone.

The first thing to understand is that the prairie is a character. Not a backdrop. It breathes. It punishes. It gives just enough to keep someone hoping—and takes just enough to keep them scared. Whether your story is set during a harsh winter, a summer drought, or a locust swarm tearing through crops, the prairie isn't just a setting. It's the test. Ask ChatGPT: *"Describe a summer on the prairie during a drought, from the perspective of a farmer's wife."* You'll get a voice full of longing, fear, and grit. That's the emotional heartbeat of your survival story.

Characters in prairie survival stories aren't always gunslingers or outlaws. They're farmers, ranchers, homesteaders, women with children and no husband, or young men too green to know what they're up against. Their enemies aren't always people—they're the elements, the land, the quiet. Use a prompt like: *"Create a character who is trying to survive alone on a prairie homestead after their family dies from illness."* That's not melodrama. That's a reality hundreds lived. And when told right, it becomes deeply powerful.

You can let survival show itself through small moments. A woman patches a torn boot with thread made from her own hair. A boy spends three days trying to trap a rabbit and fails. A man buries his only horse and starts walking. These aren't side scenes—they're the story. Ask ChatGPT: *"Describe the daily routine of someone trying to stay alive alone on the prairie with minimal resources."* What comes back won't be flashy, but it'll be real. And real hits hard.

There's also the mental and emotional toll. Being isolated in a vast landscape with no sound but wind can wear a person down faster than hunger. People start talking to the sky, seeing things in the distance that aren't there, remembering voices they'll never hear again. This psychological pressure is where a prairie survival story deepens. You're not just watching a body try to stay alive—you're watching a mind try not to break. Try a prompt like: *"Write a monologue of a prairie woman talking to her dead husband as she decides whether to abandon the farm."* That kind of writing doesn't just show survival—it *feels* it.

Survival stories also offer the chance to explore relationships in extreme conditions. A father and daughter stuck alone in a blizzard. Two strangers forced to share a dugout during a dust storm. A woman caring for a wounded man she found half-dead near the well. In these stories, trust isn't automatic. Every decision carries risk. Ask ChatGPT: *"Write a tense scene where two characters must decide whether to share their last water on the prairie."* That moment becomes a test—not just of survival, but of character.

Use the environment for pacing. Storms build tension. Animal tracks hint at hope. A fire on the horizon might mean rescue—or ruin. Every detail in a survival story should point toward a question: *Will they make it?* The answer doesn't have to be yes. But the fight to survive has to matter. Use ChatGPT to shape the stakes: *"Create a survival-based Western plot where the land becomes the main antagonist."* You'll get story arcs that don't rely on bandits or outlaws—but on nature itself.

One way to keep a prairie survival story moving is through the structure of time. It can be linear—day after day—or broken up by flashbacks, letters, or journal entries. The slow passage of time adds weight. You can also use the changing seasons. A spring storm kills the livestock. A summer drought ruins the crops. A fall freeze traps someone on the wrong side of the river. Winter? Winter can kill. Ask ChatGPT: *"Describe a prairie winter night through the eyes of someone with no firewood left."* The response will give you a scene of quiet desperation and maybe the spark of courage.

You can also bring survival stories to life through symbolism. A cracked teacup becomes a reminder of home. A buried locket keeps someone grounded. A single blooming flower in the grass signals the first real hope. These details don't just decorate your story—they give it meaning. Ask: *"List symbolic objects that can represent survival, resilience, or loss in a prairie setting."* Choose one. Build a scene around it. Let it speak when your character can't.

And don't forget: sometimes survival isn't noble. It can be ugly. People steal. People betray. People give up. That, too, is part of the story. The prairie doesn't care about honor. It cares about what works. Let your characters wrestle with hard choices. Let them regret things. Let them surprise themselves. Ask ChatGPT: *"Write a scene where a character does something morally questionable to stay alive."* You might not like what happens. But it'll be honest.

At the core of every prairie survival story is the simple, brutal question: *what does it take to keep going when there's nothing left?* And the answer is different for every character. Some fight. Some fade. Some survive—but leave part of themselves behind in the process. That's the story. Not survival for survival's sake—but what it costs, what it teaches, and what it means when someone finally sees the edge of the horizon and keeps walking.

So use the prairie. Let it stretch wide and silent and endless. Let your characters feel small in the face of it—but never helpless. Use ChatGPT to explore their thoughts, their fears, their memories. Let the struggle shape them. Let the silence speak.

Because out on the prairie, where the sky meets the land and the wind never quits, survival isn't just a fight—it's a reckoning. And those who endure don't just live. They carry the story forward.

How to Use ChatGPT for Historical Accuracy

Writing Western drama isn't just about telling a great story—it's about grounding that story in a world that feels real. A place where the dust sticks, the guns jam, and the people act and speak in ways that reflect the 19th century frontier experience. That's where historical accuracy comes in. It doesn't mean every detail must be perfect, but the *feeling* of truth must ride strong. And when you're writing fast—especially a full book, short story, or screenplay in a day—ChatGPT becomes an indispensable partner for digging up facts, checking authenticity, and building worlds that feel lived-in, not imagined.

Start with the basics. Let's say you're writing a scene in 1875 Wyoming. Before diving into dialogue or action, ask ChatGPT: *"What was life like in 1875 Wyoming?"* You'll get context—what the territory looked like, what people wore, how they traveled, what law enforcement was like, who was there before settlers arrived, and what tensions were simmering. It gives you a foundation to build scenes that don't just work—they belong in that time and place.

When you write about guns, for instance, don't just say "a revolver." Say what kind. The Colt Single Action Army was introduced in 1873 and quickly became the standard. Ask ChatGPT: *"What types of revolvers were used by lawmen and outlaws in the 1870s?"* You'll get a list with details about weight, capacity, and reliability. And then you can make that knowledge work for your story. Maybe the gun jams. Maybe your character uses a rarer model. Maybe the gun is older, passed down from a soldier in the Civil War. That single fact adds years of invisible weight to a character.

Same goes for clothing. You don't want your characters dressed like Halloween costumes. You want accuracy, even in style. Ask ChatGPT: *"What would a frontier woman wear in a prairie town in the 1880s?"* You'll learn about calico dresses, corsets, aprons, bonnets—practical clothing with layers shaped by the weather and work. You don't have to describe every detail, but knowing what they wore helps you write scenes where someone adjusts a shawl, removes their boots, or stitches a torn hem. Real things. Real people.

If you're writing a Native American character or story arc, this is where historical accuracy becomes even more essential. You need to know not just the tribe, but their location, customs, language, and historical experience during the time you're writing. Ask ChatGPT: *"What was the status of the Comanche people in Texas in the 1870s?"* The answer will give you context for their interactions with settlers, the U.S. government, the military, and each other. This allows you to write with respect and specificity, not generalizations or clichés.

Food is another powerful detail. What did they eat? What could they cook with what they had? What was a luxury and what was survival? Ask: *"What would a typical meal look like on a cattle drive in 1880?"* Suddenly your character isn't just eating "food"—he's chewing tough salt pork, soaking beans over a campfire, maybe dreaming of coffee that's more grit than grind. Small details like that build immersion fast.

You can also use ChatGPT to double-check what *didn't* exist. Want your characters to send a telegram? Make sure the line had reached their town. Want them to ride a train? Ask what railroads were active in that year and where they ran. Ask ChatGPT: *"Were there rail lines to Arizona Territory in 1882?"* The answer helps you avoid anachronisms and plot holes. A historically accurate mistake—like a railroad line that didn't exist or a word that wasn't used yet—can break the illusion for readers who know their history.

And don't forget the political and social landscape. Was there a war just ended? Was there a land rush about to begin? What was the law like? Who had power? Ask: *"What were the major issues facing settlers in Kansas in the*

1870s?" Knowing what's happening in the background can help you decide what's happening in your story. Maybe your characters are fighting over water rights, Native land treaties, or cattle barons moving into their valley.

Even weather can be historically grounded. Ask: *"What was the weather like during the winter of 1886 in Montana?"* You'll learn that it was one of the harshest winters in Western history. Ranchers lost thousands of cattle. It devastated the livestock industry. Imagine setting your story in the middle of that. Suddenly, it's not just about survival—it's about historical catastrophe.

When writing Western dialogue, you can even ask ChatGPT for era-specific language: *"Give me slang terms used in frontier towns in the 1880s."* Now your characters don't just speak—they *sound* like they came from somewhere real. Terms like "dry gulch," "calaboose," "greenhorn," or "highfalutin" have flavor and authenticity that makes your scenes richer and more believable.

Even money matters. What did a dollar buy in 1870? How much was a horse, a room at a boarding house, a bottle of whiskey? Ask: *"How much would a lawman earn in a month in the 1880s?"* The answer grounds the stakes. If your character robs a bank for $100, that's not just a chunk of change—it's possibly a year's wages. That kind of accuracy brings gravity to decisions, crimes, and risks.

Using ChatGPT to fact-check, verify, and dig deeper while you write allows you to keep momentum without sacrificing authenticity. You can write faster, knowing you're not just inventing the West—you're tapping into its bones. You don't need to be a historian. You just need to be curious. Let ChatGPT be your assistant researcher, your quick-check encyclopaedia, and your generator of period-specific color and texture.

Because writing Western drama means honoring the myth, yes—but also the people who actually lived, loved, struggled, and died under those wide-open skies. Accuracy doesn't weigh your story down—it gives it legs to stand on. It makes your world breathe.

And when your reader finishes that last page and says, *"That felt real,"* you'll know why. You took the time to get it right. And with ChatGPT's help, you didn't have to do it alone.

Mining Towns and Muddy Streets: Bringing It to Life

There's a distinct feel to a Western mining town that sets it apart from a sleepy prairie settlement or a cattle-drive outpost. It's not just the clatter of pickaxes or the flicker of lanterns in deep shafts—it's the constant sense of tension. A mining town lives on borrowed time. It's built fast, crowded tight, and always just one cave-in, one price drop, or one drunken dispute away from collapse. And when it rains, those streets turn to rivers of mud thick enough to swallow a boot and a man's pride. Writing this kind of place means capturing more than the setting. It means channeling the ambition, desperation, greed, and grime that made these towns pulse like living beasts.

When you write a mining town, start with how it was built—quick, crude, and opportunistic. Most sprang up almost overnight, chasing veins of gold, silver, or coal. Buildings were made from whatever could be hauled in fast: green lumber, canvas, salvaged boards. Streets were dirt, maybe with a bit of gravel thrown down by the few who gave a damn. The saloon and the assay office were usually the first to rise, followed by gambling dens, brothels, and general stores. Ask ChatGPT: *"Describe a mining boomtown in Colorado in the 1870s."* You'll get a place held together by ambition, sweat, and a whole lot of nails hammered in sideways.

Mud becomes a character in these towns. After a rain, the streets turn into sucking swamps of clay and horse droppings. People fall, wagons stall, tempers flare. Writing the mud isn't just for effect—it's a metaphor. No matter how shiny someone's boots, they end up caked. No matter how high a man climbs, he has to walk through the same mess as everyone else. Ask ChatGPT: *"Describe the daily experience of walking through a muddy mining town after a week of rain."* That kind of sensory detail makes your setting live in the reader's bones.

The people are what make the town tick—and tick loudly. Miners, gamblers, barkeeps, madams, widows, speculators, and pickpockets. The population was overwhelmingly male, rowdy, and fueled by liquor, labor, and long odds. But that doesn't mean there weren't complex relationships. A woman running a boarding house might know more about everyone's business than the sheriff. A child born to a Chinese miner and a local seamstress might be the first thread of something more permanent in a place meant to be temporary. Ask ChatGPT: *"Create a cast of characters who live in a frontier mining town, each with their own secrets and ambitions."* From there, the stories practically write themselves.

The rhythm of life was brutal. Miners worked sunup to sundown, often by candlelight, deep underground. Explosions, gas pockets, and collapses were common. The few who struck it rich rarely stayed rich. More often, a man would find enough to keep him going just a little longer—and that was the trap. He'd never leave. Writing a miner means writing about hope and ruin living in the same breath. Ask: *"Write an internal monologue from a miner who thinks he's found a gold vein but isn't sure if it's real."* That scene becomes about more than gold—it becomes about belief.

Danger was everywhere in a mining town. Fights broke out fast. Guns settled arguments that shovels couldn't. The law, if it existed, was often outnumbered and underpaid. Justice came quick and rough. That made these towns fertile ground for outlaws hiding in plain sight, or for someone with a past trying to bury it beneath a new name. Ask ChatGPT: *"Write a tense saloon scene in a mining town where a fugitive is recognized by a newcomer."* Now you've got drama crackling through every word.

The economy of a mining town was volatile. The local currency could be dust in a pouch or a claim staked with more hope than truth. Assayers could make or break reputations. Fake gold, rigged scales, and land disputes were common. If you want your story to feel real, have your characters talk about claim-jumping, bad ore, or a delayed shipment of blasting powder. Ask ChatGPT: *"Explain how claims were staked, worked, and defended in an 1880s mining town."* That knowledge lets you write scenes full of pressure, risk, and consequences.

You can also build depth by exploring who wasn't welcome—or who was forced to stay silent. Many mining towns had a large number of immigrant workers: Chinese, Irish, Mexican, and Black laborers who did the hardest work for the least pay. Racism and segregation were common, but so were unexpected alliances and quiet rebellions. Ask ChatGPT: *"Describe the life of a Chinese miner in a hostile Western town, and how he survives day to day."* These stories don't just add texture—they restore missing voices.

Don't forget how the town sounds. The clank of hammers. The hiss of steam engines. The distant rumble of a controlled blast. The off-key piano leaking out of the saloon. The voices shouting over one another as deals are struck, bets are lost, and someone gets tossed through swinging doors. Ask: *"Write a paragraph describing the morning noise in a busy mining town."* That soundscape pulls your readers into the street alongside your characters.

When you're ready to zoom in on a specific scene, the details will do the work. A man pulling off muddy boots at the door of a brothel. A miner pouring gold dust onto a scale and holding his breath. A woman counting coins behind a bar as a gunfight starts outside. These are the moments that let your readers live in the town, not just look at it. Ask ChatGPT: *"Describe a rainy evening in a frontier mining town where tensions are high and something is about to explode."* That prompt alone could spark a chapter, a story, or a whole screenplay.

In the end, a mining town in a Western story is more than grit and gold. It's a powder keg of people trying to get rich, trying to survive, trying to escape something behind them or reach something they've never had. And in the middle of all that, the rain falls, the mud rises, and the streets swallow another pair of boots.

Use ChatGPT to dig into those stories. Build the noise, the smells, the heartbreak. Let the mud cling to your characters until you—and your reader—can't help but believe this place was real.

Because when the town's running on luck and whiskey, and everything could fall apart by sunrise, that's where your Western finds its pulse. That's where it comes alive.

Telling the Story through Scars and Dust

In a Western, not all stories are told with words. Some are carved into flesh and written in the dirt. A scar running from a man's collarbone to his jaw. A worn rifle with initials etched into the stock. A pair of boots cracked from too many miles in the desert. These aren't props. They're history. And when you learn to tell your story through scars and dust, you're writing in the true language of the frontier—quiet, brutal, honest. This is where your characters come alive without ever needing to say what happened. The evidence is already there.

A scar tells you who someone is before they speak. A jagged mark down a gunfighter's back? That wasn't from a duel—it was from running, maybe losing. A stitched line above a woman's eye? Maybe she fought back. Maybe she still does. A missing finger, a healed bullet wound, a limp—these are all narrative threads waiting to be tugged. When you use scars in your storytelling, you're letting the past speak through the body. You can ask ChatGPT: *"Describe the physical appearance of a Western character whose past can be read in his scars."* What comes back is usually more revealing than any backstory monologue ever could be.

Don't just describe a scar—*show what it does.* Does the man rub it when he's nervous? Does the woman keep hers hidden until she's ready to tell the truth? Does a young cowboy ask how someone got it, and the room goes silent? These are your storytelling moments. They don't interrupt the narrative—they *are* the narrative. Try a prompt like: *"Write a Western scene where two characters bond while revealing their scars."* What unfolds will likely carry more intimacy than a dozen conversations.

And then there's the dust. It's not just something on the boots—it's everywhere. It's in the lungs, in the eyes, in the folds of clothing. It settles on gravestones and forgotten dreams. Dust in a Western is symbolic. It means age, abandonment, hardship, distance, silence. It means time has passed and nothing's been cleaned or fixed. When you set a story in dust, you're grounding it in a world where survival means being dirty, worn, and weathered.

Ask ChatGPT: *"Describe a Western town choked with dust after weeks without rain."* What you'll get isn't just a setting—it's a tone. A story where people squint, cough, and keep moving even though their skin's cracking and their livestock are dying. A story where the dust becomes part of the people—just like their scars.

You can use dust to reveal state of mind. A man who never brushes it off his coat might be too tired to care. A woman who fights to keep her windows clean in a dusty town might be clinging to something deeper—hope, pride, control. A child drawing in the dust might be the last moment of innocence before the story changes. Prompt ChatGPT: *"Write a quiet scene in which a character reflects while wiping dust from a mirror."* You'll see how powerful stillness can be in a Western.

Scars and dust are also great tools for subtext. You don't have to explain what happened in the past—you just need to show what's left of it. A man who flinches when someone slaps him on the back. A woman who touches the dust-covered gravestone of a brother who never came home. You can trust your audience to fill in the gaps. And ChatGPT can help you explore those silent beats: *"Create a dialogue-free scene in which two characters recognize they share a painful past."*

Sometimes the story is told in what the dust has *covered.* A revolver found under floorboards. A photograph in a drawer. A wedding dress that's turned the color of bone. What was buried or forgotten now becomes part of the story's turning point. That moment when someone kicks through the dust and finds something that changes everything. Ask: *"Write a Western scene where a character discovers something important in a long-abandoned house."* You'll find that the setting does as much storytelling as the people.

Even how a character *moves* through the dust and what they do with their scars gives you insight. Do they walk heavy, not caring who hears? Do they limp, try to hide the injury? Do they dust off their hat before entering the saloon—or leave the layer of dust as a warning that they've come from far away? These choices say everything. Ask ChatGPT: *"Describe a gunslinger entering a town for the first time in weeks of hard travel."* You'll feel the weariness in every step.

When writing in this way, the beauty of the Western comes through its restraint. You don't have to explain. You show. A backstory becomes a glance at a scar. A broken heart becomes a dusty letter never sent. A dream dies when someone looks up at the sky and says nothing. The more you lean into that kind of storytelling, the more your world feels true.

And scars aren't always on skin. They're in the land—burned trees, half-built homes, old fence posts buried in weeds. They're in the towns—bullet holes in walls, graves with no names, saloons that never laugh like they used to. Scars and dust tell you this land has been lived in. That it has a memory. That your story is just one of many riding across the surface.

So when you use ChatGPT while writing, don't just ask for backstory. Ask for marks. Ask for what's left behind. Prompt: *"What physical or environmental details can show a character's past without dialogue?"* The answers will help you write with layers—where every scar is a sentence, every layer of dust a page.

Because in a Western, it's not what they say that tells the story.

It's what's written on their skin.

It's what settles in the silence.

It's the scars and the dust.

And in the end, that's where the truth always waits.

Children of the Frontier: Youth in the West

The frontier was a harsh place to grow up. Childhood in the West wasn't about innocence—it was about endurance. The wide-open landscapes, the dangerous trails, the isolation, and the constant push to survive shaped the youngest lives just as much as the adults'. If you want your Western story to feel real and grounded, don't forget the children. They were there, playing in the dirt outside the general store, hauling water from the well, watching with wide eyes as gunmen passed by and violence broke out. The frontier didn't spare them—it shaped them. And telling their stories, or even weaving them into the background of your drama, adds texture, vulnerability, and humanity to your tale.

Western stories often sideline kids or reduce them to background props, but children on the frontier were never passive. They worked the land. They cared for siblings. They rode horses, fetched firewood, helped birth animals, learned to shoot. They knew things they shouldn't, and sometimes they grew up too fast. Ask ChatGPT: *"Describe the daily life of a 10-year-old living on a frontier homestead in 1880."* What you get will not be idle play. It'll be chores, responsibility, moments of quiet rebellion, and the sharp edge of childhood under pressure.

Boys and girls both had roles to play, but they often learned to blur the lines. A girl might wear her brother's boots and sneak off to help drive cattle. A boy might be expected to shoot a wolf at twelve, even if his hands were still shaking from the sound of his father's anger the night before. Survival didn't care about gender norms—it cared about results. A child who could trap a rabbit, aim a rifle, or mend a shirt was valuable, regardless of age or gender. Use ChatGPT to explore this dynamic: *"Create a character sketch of a teenage girl who dresses as a boy to work a job on the frontier."* That story will immediately carry tension, secrecy, and purpose.

The emotional lives of frontier children are often overlooked—but they're rich with possibility. Loneliness, longing, fear, and fierce attachment to small things—a wooden toy, a tattered book, a loyal dog—these were the ways children found meaning in a harsh world. They also served as mirrors to the adult characters. A hardened outlaw might soften when faced with a child's trust. A tough rancher might see their own lost youth in the eyes of a local orphan. Ask ChatGPT: *"Write a quiet Western scene between a gunfighter and a child who doesn't understand what he's done."* That kind of encounter can reveal more about both characters than pages of exposition.

Orphaned children were a common part of the West. Illness, accidents, raids, and violence left many young ones alone or taken in by others. You can write from that perspective, giving a child's view of events that adults rationalize or avoid. A kid doesn't always understand everything, but they *feel* it. The fear. The hunger. The silence. Ask: *"Write a scene from the point of view of a frontier orphan watching a stranger arrive in town."* The vulnerability in that voice can ground your story in ways that nothing else can.

Children also absorb the values of the world around them. If the town reveres violence, they grow up idolizing guns. If the adults around them are bitter or broken, they learn to shield themselves early. But they also carry hope. A child on the frontier might believe that tomorrow could still be better. That's the heart of their power in a story—not just vulnerability, but possibility. Ask ChatGPT: *"Create a dialogue between two frontier children imagining what their town will look like when they grow up."* That moment of dreaming in a world that often crushes dreams can be striking.

Education, too, plays into the story. Some towns had one-room schoolhouses, others had nothing at all. A child might know how to read because their mother taught them by firelight, or they might never hold a book in their life. But stories traveled, even without paper. Folklore, tall tales, ghost stories—they passed from mouth to mouth, especially among kids. Use this in your story by asking: *"List folktales or superstitions that children might whisper to each other in an*

1870s Western town." These can add atmosphere and tradition, and show how even young minds tried to make sense of a chaotic world.

Friendships between children on the frontier were often forged fast and held tight. A neighbor's child could become a sibling in spirit. Shared chores, whispered secrets, and stolen games in the tall grass created strong bonds. But these friendships were also tested—by distance, family feuds, and sudden tragedy. Ask ChatGPT: *"Write a Western scene where two childhood friends are forced to say goodbye as one family leaves town."* That kind of emotional weight, from a child's perspective, hits in a different way.

Children also witnessed more than they should. They saw death. They heard gunshots. They watched their parents suffer. Some were scarred by what they couldn't unsee. Others became stoic, strong, and fiercely loyal. You can write a child character who seems calm—but whose silence holds a storm. Ask: *"Create a Western story where a child silently seeks revenge for their parent's death."* That's a story with darkness, but also clarity—because children often see truth without the filters adults wear.

In a screenplay, children in Westerns can create stark visual contrasts. A little girl in a white dress walking through a burned-out town. A young boy playing marbles in the dirt outside a saloon. These images don't need dialogue—they carry meaning just by existing. They remind the audience that even in a violent, adult world, youth endures—and sometimes, it watches closely.

And sometimes, children are the reason a character changes. The outlaw who gives up violence. The drunk who finds purpose. The lawman who stops running. A child can be the moral compass, the turning point, the unexpected reason for someone to keep going. But be careful—don't use them as tools or tropes. Make them real. Make them messy. Let them cry, lie, laugh, and surprise you.

Because the children of the frontier weren't just part of the West—they *were* the West. They carried it forward. They adapted, endured, and became the next generation of settlers, dreamers, gunslingers, and peacekeepers. They were shaped by the dust and the hardship, but also by the stars overhead and the stories told by firelight.

So when you use ChatGPT to build your cast, don't forget the kids. Ask the questions. Dig into their fears and their fun. Show the prairie through their eyes. Because when you let them speak, even in whispers, they'll bring a whole new kind of truth to your Western.

After all, it's not just the hardened riders who define the frontier.

It's the barefoot child running beside them.

Watching. Learning.

And becoming.

How to Weave Multiple Character Arcs Together

A Western isn't just about one person riding into the sunset. It's about a town, a trail, a conflict that ripples through many lives at once. A great Western drama feels big because it moves through a web of characters—some working together, some colliding, and some never even speaking but still shaping the same storm. When you know how to weave multiple character arcs together, your story becomes richer, deeper, and far more satisfying. And if you're using ChatGPT to help structure those arcs, you'll find it's like laying track for a train with many cars, all heading toward one final destination.

It starts with knowing that not every character's arc has to be loud or dramatic. Some are small and subtle—a shift in belief, a single decision that changes the course of a life. Others are grand: the outlaw turned hero, the lawman turned broken, the townsperson who finally takes a stand. When weaving multiple arcs, you want contrast. A character on a redemptive journey plays beautifully against someone on a downward spiral. A young girl discovering her courage might sit in emotional opposition to a gunslinger losing his nerve. Ask ChatGPT: *"Create three Western characters with opposing emotional arcs that intersect in a single story."* The differences between them will create natural tension.

Now, to weave those arcs, you need a shared world that forces interaction. A town on the edge of collapse. A land war between cattle barons and farmers. A bounty posted for a man no one agrees on. Let the setting be the rope that ties them together. They don't all need to share the same screen or page at the same time, but their choices should affect one another. One man's failure to act might cause another's rise. One woman's secret might lead to another's downfall. Ask: *"Describe a Western scenario that connects five characters through one unfolding crisis."* From there, you're not juggling characters—you're threading a story.

Timing is everything. Each arc needs moments to breathe. Don't pile them all into one chapter or scene. Instead, structure your story like a braid—moving from one character to the next, returning again with each new stage of their journey. This builds rhythm and gives your audience time to emotionally invest. Use ChatGPT to help pace it: *"Outline a Western story where three character arcs unfold over a shared timeline."* The output can serve as your roadmap, showing where each thread enters and exits.

To keep the arcs connected, give your characters shared emotional themes even if their goals are different. Maybe they're all wrestling with legacy. Or identity. Or the question of justice versus revenge. This creates resonance even when their actions diverge. A preacher might wrestle with forgiveness at the same time an ex-con is trying to atone for past sins. Their methods differ, but their internal battles mirror each other. Prompt ChatGPT: *"Develop two Western characters whose arcs contrast in action but align in theme."* This makes your story feel cohesive without forcing character interactions that feel unnatural.

Another trick to weaving arcs is the ripple effect. One character's decision should shape another's journey, even if indirectly. A saloon girl decides to leave town—her absence leaves the sheriff isolated. A boy loses his dog to a wandering outlaw—he grows up to hunt him down. These aren't separate arcs; they're linked by cause and consequence. Use a prompt like: *"Write a sequence of cause-and-effect events across multiple Western character arcs."* This structure keeps your plot alive with motion and tension.

You can also use objects or events as anchors. A buried treasure. A single gun. A letter written and passed from hand to hand. These become narrative threads that travel across arcs, connecting characters who may never meet but who are all affected by the same thing. Ask: *"List objects or shared events that could connect five characters in a Western drama."* These items give your story a totem, something physical to track emotional movement.

When arcs do intersect, make those meetings count. Let characters reflect each other's change. Let the quiet girl who once feared everything stand between two killers. Let the wounded lawman who gave up the badge meet the outlaw who took it from him. These aren't just confrontations—they're payoffs. Use ChatGPT to help script these moments: *"Write a dialogue scene where two Western characters with opposing arcs confront one another."* These scenes are the campfires where your entire plot glows brightest.

Each arc also needs its own ending—success, failure, or ambiguity. But they should all resolve around the same time, like instruments finishing a song together. One may die, another may ride off, another may find peace—but the emotional note they strike should harmonize. You can prompt ChatGPT: *"Create three character resolutions that reflect the same theme but in different outcomes."* That kind of unified ending brings deep satisfaction to your reader.

And don't forget that some arcs are incomplete on purpose. Some characters stay lost. Some never find redemption. Some pass the baton to the next generation. The town drunk doesn't sober up—but his daughter becomes the town's first schoolteacher. The gunfighter doesn't hang up his revolver—but he spares the kid who reminds him of himself. These echoes stretch the narrative beyond the page, making the story feel larger than itself. Ask: *"Describe a Western story with legacy-based character arcs spanning generations."*

If you're writing a novel, use chapters to shift perspective. If it's a screenplay, use scenes and visual cues—posture, props, clothing—to show emotional change. Let ChatGPT help you track this with prompts like: *"Build a scene list showing each character's turning point in a Western drama."* That list can keep you from losing the thread, ensuring that each arc lands where it needs to.

Ultimately, weaving multiple arcs is about empathy and precision. You're building an emotional ecosystem. Everyone wants something. Everyone is changing. And they're all part of the same world, breathing the same dust, watching the same sun go down.

And when it all comes together—when the arcs rise and fall, collide and echo, lift and break—you don't just have a Western.

You have a world that feels alive.

A story that belongs to everyone in it.

And a chorus of characters all riding toward the same horizon—whether they know it or not.

Writing the Train Heist, Bank Robbery, or Stagecoach Hold-up

No Western is complete without at least one moment of sheer outlaw audacity. The train heist, the bank robbery, the stagecoach hold-up—these are staples of the genre, explosive turning points in the narrative that do more than deliver action. They reveal character, raise stakes, and unleash consequences that echo long after the smoke clears. But writing these scenes well isn't just about gunfire and shouting. It's about planning, pacing, personality, and how the violence reveals what your characters are really made of. These events are loud chapters in stories built on quiet choices—and when done right, they can define the entire narrative.

Let's start with the train heist. It's the most cinematic of the three and usually the most ambitious. A train heist is moving chaos. It takes strategy, guts, and nerves. You've got speed, momentum, guards, passengers, and tight spaces. Whether your characters are robbing a payroll car, rescuing a prisoner, or stealing something bigger—like a ledger of land deeds or stolen military documents—the train itself becomes a character. It groans, shakes, and thunders across the landscape, challenging your characters at every turn. Ask ChatGPT: *"Describe a train robbery in a Western from the perspective of a nervous but skilled newcomer to the gang."* You'll get tension, detail, and emotion that pull you deeper than just the action.

When writing the mechanics of a train heist, you need to think about how your crew boards it—do they jump from horses? Lie in wait at a canyon curve? Climb aboard in disguise at the last town stop? Every choice changes the tone of the scene. A subtle infiltration sets up suspense. A full-frontal assault starts with a bang. Ask ChatGPT: *"List different ways outlaws could rob a moving train in the 1880s."* Pick one that fits your crew's personalities and strengths.

Now the bank robbery—this one hits closer to town and to the heart. It's not just about the money. It's about territory, risk, power. Robbing a bank means challenging the order of the town. The sheriff. The townsfolk. The banker who thought his vault was untouchable. A robbery scene here can turn on dialogue—on a threat whispered over a counter, a teller's trembling hand, a vault door that won't open fast enough. Ask ChatGPT: *"Write a Western bank robbery scene where one of the robbers is secretly having doubts."* That gives you a layered moment where tension builds not only from the situation, but from inside the group.

Banks aren't just about what's in the safe. They're about who's watching. Who's willing to resist. Who freezes. Who fires. A bystander with a shotgun. A child hiding under the desk. A deputy who wasn't supposed to be on shift. These are the surprises that make the robbery go wrong—or reveal the real strength of your characters. Ask: *"Describe a bank robbery from the perspective of a silent bystander who suddenly acts."* The lens doesn't have to be on the outlaws for the story to hit hard.

And then there's the stagecoach hold-up. This one is a little more intimate, a little more personal. There are fewer moving parts but more human reactions. A coach might carry payroll, jewelry, mail—or something more valuable, like a witness, a prisoner, or a map. Your characters might wear masks, or maybe they don't care about being recognized. Maybe it's their first job. Maybe it's their last. What makes a stagecoach scene sing is the suddenness—one moment a journey, the next, ambush. Use a prompt like: *"Write a Western stagecoach robbery in which the lead robber recognizes someone inside."* Suddenly the crime turns into a personal reckoning.

These scenes aren't just action—they're decisions. Does the outlaw shoot or show mercy? Does the guard drop his weapon or fight back? Does the town turn a blind eye—or take up arms? The robbery is the ignition. What follows is the fire. And your story can use these moments to splinter relationships, start manhunts, or reveal someone's true face.

You can explore that with ChatGPT: *"Create a Western plot where a robbery gone wrong tears a gang apart."* That gives you aftermath to work with—always more important than the act itself.

Pacing is critical. A robbery shouldn't drag, but it shouldn't rush either. Build the anticipation. The planning. The tension in the eyes of the characters before they burst into the bank, leap onto the train, or block the road with rifles drawn. Make the reader *wait* for the first shout or the first shot. Use ChatGPT to craft the pacing: *"Outline the beats of a high-stakes robbery scene in a Western film."* Each beat gives you a moment to raise the stakes.

And don't forget the environment. A dusty street in the heat of noon. A dark train tunnel where everything could go wrong. A canyon where a stagecoach can't turn back. These settings trap your characters. They focus the action. Ask ChatGPT: *"Describe a robbery setting in a Western that adds danger or complication."* Then make the scene lean into that setting's specific danger.

A good Western heist scene ends with more questions than answers. Did they get what they came for? Did they leave someone behind? Is someone bleeding, or missing, or whispering a betrayal? Use those outcomes to launch the next act. Maybe the outlaw starts to question the life. Maybe the sheriff vows to hunt them to the ends of the territory. Maybe a kid who watched from the saloon window decides to follow them next time. Ask: *"What are five narrative consequences that can follow a Western heist gone wrong?"* Pick one. Or pick all five.

Whether it's a train, a bank, or a stagecoach, the robbery scene isn't just about the take—it's about the toll. On the robbers. On the victims. On the town. On the story. These scenes don't just give you action—they give you fractures. And from those fractures, your characters have to rebuild. Or collapse.

So let the bullets fly. Let the vault burst open. Let the horses run. But don't stop there.

Because the West always remembers who took what—and who paid the price.

The Ranch, the Range, and the Reckoning

The Western isn't all duels and dust. Sometimes it's sweat, soil, and sunrise. It's the creak of a barn door, the call of cattle at dawn, and the smell of horses and hay mixed with gun oil and bad coffee. The ranch and the open range form the spine of the Western frontier. This is where the battle for land, legacy, and manhood takes root—quietly at first, but always leading to a reckoning. Writing the ranch and the range into your story grounds the drama in something real and elemental: work. Labor. Blood passed down through fences, and grudges that ride as long as the herd.

The ranch is more than a home—it's a fortress, a symbol, a line in the sand. It's the dream every character either wants, protects, or steals. For one man, it's his father's land. For another, it's a prize to take by force. For a woman, it may be the only independence she's ever known. Use ChatGPT to set the tone: *"Describe a family-run cattle ranch in 1880s New Mexico Territory that has survived two generations of hardship."* What you get won't just be buildings and fences. It'll be scars in the land and ghosts in the hallways.

Daily life on the ranch is brutal and repetitive—branding, herding, fencing, calving, mending what the weather and time try to break. And yet, there's beauty in that grind. A sunrise after a long rain. A horse that finally trusts its rider. A moment of stillness before the dust is kicked up again. Ask: *"Write a morning on a Western ranch through the eyes of someone who doesn't know if they'll keep it another year."* That kind of character perspective brings tension even when no one's drawn a gun.

The range, meanwhile, is freedom and danger all at once. It's the open wild, the place where cattle graze and cowhands disappear. This is where conflicts brew—between ranchers and sheep herders, settlers and speculators, homesteaders and barons. Water rights. Fencing disputes. Grazing wars. These weren't just politics—they were gunfights waiting to happen. Prompt ChatGPT: *"Explain the tensions between cattle ranchers and homesteaders in the 1880s Western frontier."* That will give your story a wider context to anchor your personal arcs in.

The reckoning, though—it's never just about one incident. It builds. Maybe it starts when a fence goes up across an old trail. Maybe when a neighbor's cattle go missing. Maybe when the railroad comes, and someone signs over land without telling the rest. The reckoning is when silence runs out. It's the moment the rancher puts down the branding iron and picks up the rifle. It's when a son stands up to his father. It's when the range becomes a battleground. You can ask ChatGPT: *"Write the turning point in a Western story where a quiet rancher decides to fight for his land."* That's the kind of emotional shift that drives the last act of a great Western.

Ranch life also invites intergenerational drama. A father and son at odds over how to run the place. A daughter who wants to take over but faces resistance. A grandfather who remembers when the land was won with blood and doesn't trust anyone who didn't bleed for it. Use a prompt like: *"Create a conflict between three generations of ranchers over the future of the land."* That gives your story internal stakes that don't need a single shot fired—just a sharp word, a broken promise, a betrayal over breakfast.

Don't forget the animals. The cattle are more than background—they're the business, the burden, the blessing. Losing a calf can mean ruin. A stampede can mean death. A dry season might mean selling off the herd, or watching them die under a hot, empty sky. Horses are companions, tools, and lifelines. A man's bond with his horse says more than his words ever could. Ask: *"Describe the emotional connection between a rancher and a horse he raised from birth."* That's the kind of moment that reveals the soul of the character without a speech.

Weather is another force that shapes everything. A hard winter. A spring flood. A summer of heat and grassfires. These aren't just backdrops—they're antagonists. Ask ChatGPT: *"Write a scene where a rancher fights to save his herd during a flash flood."* You'll find the drama doesn't need outlaws when the land itself is a threat.

The reckoning, when it comes, doesn't have to be a gunfight—but it often is. Because in the West, justice and violence are old drinking partners. Maybe the ranch is under siege from a greedy cattle syndicate. Maybe a corrupt sheriff's trying to force a sale. Maybe it's the quiet, slow-burn feud between two neighbors that ends in blood. However it goes down, it has to feel earned. The work, the fear, the pride—let it all crash down in that final moment. Use ChatGPT to map it: *"Outline a Western story where a rancher reaches his breaking point and takes a stand."*

But not all reckoning is loud. Some is silent. A son walks away from the land. A woman buries her last cow and boards up the house. A man kneels in the dirt of a place he swore he'd never leave and weeps. These endings carry weight because they tell the truth: not every battle is won. But every battle leaves a mark. Ask: *"Write the final journal entry of a Western rancher who lost his land but not his dignity."* That's the kind of ending readers carry with them.

Because the ranch isn't just a location—it's a promise. The range isn't just land—it's legacy. And the reckoning? That's the moment when you find out what all of it was worth.

So build your fences. Ride the fence line. Brand your herd.

But always be ready—because the West remembers everything.

And out there, under that endless sky, every man, woman, and story gets called to account.

Frontier Women: Writing Strong Female Leads

In Western storytelling, the dusty myth often leans hard into the image of rugged men riding alone across wide-open spaces. But beneath the grit and gunfire, the frontier was also held together, often quietly, by the strength and resilience of women. They ran ranches, raised children, held towns together, stitched wounds, buried the dead, and stood their ground when the world tried to knock them flat. A Western without women isn't just incomplete—it's dishonest. And when you write a strong female lead, you don't have to invent one. You just have to listen to the truth the old stories ignored.

Frontier women were complex because the frontier was unforgiving. Some were born into it, some were dragged into it, and some chased it themselves. But wherever they came from, they learned fast that survival didn't care about social rules. A strong female lead in a Western doesn't always carry a rifle—though she certainly can. Sometimes her weapon is silence. Sometimes it's knowledge. Sometimes it's her refusal to leave, even when everything around her says run. You can prompt ChatGPT: *"Create a female lead in a Western who survives by intelligence, not violence."* The result might not wear a holster, but she'll still carry power.

The key to writing her well is never confusing strength with perfection. A strong frontier woman might make mistakes. She might cry. She might lose. But she gets back up. She keeps going. That's what made her strong—not that she could outshoot every man in town, but that she kept standing when life tried to flatten her. Ask ChatGPT: *"Describe a female rancher fighting to keep her land after her husband dies."* What you'll get is heart, determination, and truth—more powerful than any duel.

These women came in many forms. A schoolteacher with a shotgun hidden under her desk. A brothel madam who knows how to outwit every man who walks through her doors. A homesteader who's buried more children than she's saved, but still plants in spring. A young girl who watches, learns, and waits for her moment to speak. Each of them carries a story that belongs in the dust and sunlight of the Western frontier. Try a prompt like: *"List five archetypes for strong female characters in a Western setting."* From there, choose one—or blend them.

And don't be afraid to show how society pushed against them. The West was a world of expectations: cook, clean, serve, stay quiet. But frontier women pushed back. They sued for land rights. They refused marriages. They taught themselves to read. They fought to vote. These weren't background figures—they were often the ones who gave the town its backbone. You can write a female lead who is quiet—but still resists. You can write one who shouts. You can write one who plays by the rules long enough to change them. Ask ChatGPT: *"Write a scene in which a frontier woman confronts a town council trying to take her property."* That's the kind of story where resolve shines.

Don't reduce her to a sidekick or a love interest. Let her have her own arc. Maybe she wants to avenge something. Maybe she wants to protect someone. Maybe she just wants to live in peace and is tired of burying people she loves. The Western is a perfect genre for letting women fight, lead, run, hide, win, and lose—all on their own terms. You can ask: *"Outline a Western plot where the main character is a woman seeking justice in a lawless town."* That's not a subplot—that's a full-blown narrative with teeth.

Romance? Sure. But let it be real. Love on the frontier was hard. It had to survive isolation, hardship, distance, and the constant shadow of death. A woman might love someone and still send them away. She might choose herself. Or she might find love where she least expects it—in a traveling doctor, a wounded outlaw, or even a rival. Ask ChatGPT:

"Write a Western scene where a female lead chooses love, but on her own terms." That moment will have more weight because she earned it.

When writing strong female leads, show the small victories. The girl who rides a horse no one else could tame. The widow who builds a school in memory of her son. The mother who puts herself between danger and her child. These moments show courage without needing a shootout. And sometimes, yes—she *is* the one who draws first and shoots straight. Let her do that too.

Also consider giving her allies and enemies. Other women she leans on or clashes with. Female friendships in Westerns are rare—but powerful. A midwife and a rancher's wife. A teacher and a saloon girl. These relationships don't need to be tidy. Let them challenge each other. Let them disagree, protect, abandon, or save one another. Ask ChatGPT: *"Describe a complex relationship between two frontier women on opposite sides of the law."* That story can be as fierce and emotional as any high-stakes duel.

And when the reckoning comes—because in a Western, it always does—let her face it on her terms. Maybe she wins. Maybe she walks away. Maybe she buries the past and finally breathes. But whatever her ending is, let it belong to her. She's earned it.

Because the West wasn't just built by men on horseback.

It was built by women with dirt on their hands and fire in their hearts.

And their stories—like the land they stood on—run deeper than we ever knew.

Creating Antagonists with Depth and Danger

The Western antagonist isn't just the man in black or the gang terrorizing the town. The best ones aren't defined by their hats or their guns, but by the force they represent and the choices they make. A great antagonist in a Western drama isn't just dangerous because of what they *do*—they're dangerous because of what they *believe*, and how deeply they believe it. And if you want your story to hit hard and stick around long after the last bullet is fired, then your antagonist needs to be more than a target. They need to be a presence that shapes the story, rattles the hero, and complicates the idea of right and wrong.

Start by asking: *What is this character willing to do to get what they want?* And then go deeper: *Why do they think they're right?* Most compelling antagonists believe they're the hero of their own story. They justify cruelty with order, violence with justice, greed with survival. A land baron might see himself as the visionary modernizing the frontier. A bounty hunter might justify torture as necessary to tame lawlessness. An ex-soldier turned outlaw might still think he's fighting a war that never really ended. Ask ChatGPT: *"Create a Western antagonist who believes he's saving the town by using violent control."* That's not just a villain—it's someone who thinks he's the sheriff in a world gone mad.

Layering in a backstory adds weight to their actions. Maybe the antagonist lost family during a land grab. Maybe they were betrayed by a friend. Maybe they watched everything they loved vanish when the railroad came through. Their pain doesn't excuse what they do, but it explains why they do it. It also gives your protagonist something to react to—a reason to hesitate, to reflect, to question. Prompt ChatGPT: *"Describe a Western antagonist whose cruelty is rooted in a childhood betrayal."* You'll get a character who feels more real than just a guy with a quick draw and a sneer.

Let your antagonist be charismatic. Let them speak well. Let them hold the room. The villain who rants and raves is predictable. The one who smiles while he threatens your hero's family is unforgettable. Think about how someone like this would manipulate others, command loyalty, or stir fear. Ask ChatGPT: *"Write a scene where a Western antagonist wins over a crowd while hiding his true motives."* This kind of villain doesn't just move through the story—they *shape* it.

Another trick to writing dangerous antagonists is making them reflect the darkest parts of your protagonist. If your hero is a former outlaw trying to go straight, let the antagonist be the one who stayed crooked—and got rich doing it. If your hero is trying to live by a code, let the antagonist be the one who lost faith in codes a long time ago. This dynamic turns every encounter into a mirror. They challenge each other not just physically, but philosophically. Ask: *"Create a Western hero and villain who represent two opposing views of justice."* That tension adds meaning to every gunfight, every stare-down, every whispered threat.

Antagonists can also be part of a larger system. Maybe your villain is backed by a corrupt railroad company. Maybe he's the sheriff, the preacher, the banker—the very system your hero has to fight from within. When your antagonist isn't just a person but an *institution*, the stakes go through the roof. Suddenly your hero isn't just trying to beat one man—they're trying to survive a world designed to keep them down. Ask ChatGPT: *"Outline a Western plot where the antagonist controls the law, the land, and the town."* That kind of structure can make every scene feel like a noose tightening.

Don't forget emotional danger. The best villains don't just threaten with guns—they know what to say to unmake a person. Maybe they know a secret. Maybe they were once friends with the protagonist. Maybe they saved their life once, or betrayed them at the worst moment. These personal stakes cut deeper than any blade. Ask: *"Write a confrontation between a Western hero and an antagonist who was once his mentor."* The result won't just be dramatic—it'll be tragic, and tragedy makes for unforgettable drama.

It also helps to give your antagonist their own arc. Let them change, even if it's for the worse. Let their choices cost them. Let them struggle, doubt, lash out. They don't have to be likable—but they should be human. Maybe they fall further into darkness as they lose control. Maybe they get more brutal as their empire crumbles. Or maybe they surprise you—and the reader—by making a choice that even the hero wouldn't have predicted. Prompt ChatGPT: *"Describe a Western antagonist who has a moment of doubt before committing to a final violent act."* That's not just good character work—it's good storytelling.

Visually, your antagonist should leave a mark. A distinctive scar. A dusty suit too clean for the town. A silver cane. A calm voice. A tendency to whistle when he's about to kill. These touches become memorable, haunting, iconic. Ask: *"Give me visual traits and behaviors that make a Western villain instantly recognizable."* You can build that into your script, your novel, your storyboard—wherever you're telling your tale.

The final showdown—the reckoning—only works if the villain feels like a worthy threat. That doesn't mean they have to be stronger. It means they have to have *earned* this moment. Through fear, manipulation, destruction, or sheer nerve, they've left a trail that only the hero can answer. When you write that final scene, make it feel inevitable. Like these two were always going to meet at high noon or in a burning barn or outside the saloon while the town watches with bated breath. Ask ChatGPT: *"Write a final Western standoff between a reluctant hero and a charismatic villain with nothing left to lose."* Then tweak, refine, and deepen it until it punches like it should.

Because in the West, the villain isn't just someone to beat.

They're the shadow the hero walks through to find themselves.

The voice that calls out everything the hero might've become.

And when done right—they're the fire that makes your story burn.

The Border Town: Cultures, Crimes, and Consequences

A Western border town isn't just a line on a map—it's a place where everything bleeds together. Languages, customs, laws, dreams, and dangers. The edge of a nation and the edge of identity. North meets South. Cowboys meet vaqueros. Rebels meet outlaws. These towns are messy, beautiful, dangerous crossroads, where the gunsmoke doesn't settle easily and every story is half-told in two languages. Writing a border town means writing a place full of tension and texture, a space that holds more than just conflict—it holds contradictions.

Start by anchoring your town between two worlds. Maybe it's on the U.S.-Mexico border in the 1880s, where the Rio Grande cuts through desert and trade routes snake through outlaw country. Or maybe it's a former Mexican settlement absorbed by westward expansion, where the old mission bells still toll even as English names replace Spanish ones. These towns don't forget who they were—they carry it, quietly or defiantly. Use ChatGPT to ask: *"Describe a Western border town on the Texas-Mexico line in 1885."* You'll get a setting built on shifting loyalties and deeper history than any new sheriff can control.

Culturally, a border town pulses with dual identities. The townspeople might speak Spanish in the home and English in the saloon. The church might hold services in two languages. Food stalls serve tortillas next to salted jerky. Celebrations might mix Catholic saints with frontier grit. And while that blend creates a vibrant world, it also carries friction. Racism, assimilation, resistance, and misunderstanding all swirl in the air. Writing this means respecting that complexity. Ask ChatGPT: *"List ways Mexican and American cultures intersected in 19th-century border towns."* These aren't just set dressing—they're the heartbeat of the place.

A border town is the perfect ground for crime. Smuggling. Rustling. Gambling. Gun running. Bandits crossing at night and disappearing into the desert by morning. The local law might be outgunned, underpaid, or simply corrupt. Maybe the sheriff takes bribes to look the other way. Maybe a former revolutionary now runs the largest cantina—and nothing happens in town without his say-so. Maybe a gang uses the border as a shield, knowing the jurisdiction ends before the trail does. You can explore this by prompting: *"Create a Western border town controlled by a crime family operating on both sides of the law."*

The crime isn't just violence—it's economics. A shipment of rifles bound for rebels. A child kidnapped and ransomed across the river. A cattle deal sabotaged to collapse a rival's ranch. Every illegal act has political and personal consequences. When you write this world, every deal made should carry a price—maybe not right away, but it always comes due. Ask ChatGPT: *"Write a scene where a rancher crosses the border to strike a deal that will protect his land but endanger his soul."* That kind of tradeoff builds drama with weight.

Characters in a border town are rarely black-and-white. The schoolteacher might be the daughter of a famous bandit. The priest might have once ridden with revolutionaries. The local judge might be married to a woman from across the river—and that love may be the only reason he hasn't fled the town entirely. These people don't just live with tension—they are the tension. You can generate characters by asking: *"Create five morally complex characters who live in a Western border town."* Use them to build rivalries, secret alliances, and quiet tragedies.

Border towns are also places of escape and arrival. Refugees from war. Exiles from cities. Fugitives. Runaways. They bring stories, languages, scars, and secrets. Someone might be hiding under a new name. Someone else might be searching for the truth that drove them there. These towns are final chances and fresh starts—sometimes both. Ask: *"Write the arrival scene of a mysterious traveler in a Western border town with a hidden past."* How the town reacts tells you more than anything about who runs it—and who's afraid.

The consequences in a border town stretch further than the gunfire. When law and loyalty clash, people get caught in between. A wrong word in the wrong tongue. A deal made without understanding both sides. A shootout where the body falls on the wrong side of the border—and sparks something bigger. Writing this means letting the reader feel that constant edge, where any step might start a fire. Ask ChatGPT: *"Describe a border incident that threatens to ignite war between factions in a Western town."* That's not just plot—that's pressure.

You also have the chance to show solidarity. People from different worlds sharing water during a drought. A Mexican healer treating the sheriff's wounded son. A white rancher risking his life to stop a lynch mob targeting a friend's family. These moments carry power—not just because they're rare, but because they show what a border town *could* be, not just what it often is. Ask: *"Write a Western scene where two characters from opposing cultures protect each other during a violent uprising."* That's the soul of storytelling in a place full of ghosts and hope.

And visually, the border town is stunning. Colorful textiles hanging in the market next to dusty rifles. Sand blowing across old adobe walls. Horses tied beside carts loaded with pottery and ammunition. A cantina lit by lanterns and buzzing with music, laughter, and whispered betrayal. You can build a whole world with just one block of this town. Ask: *"Describe the central plaza of a Western border town at sunset."* You'll get texture, movement, and atmosphere.

Because in a border town, the line isn't just geographical.

It runs through every decision. Every character. Every moment.

And whether they cross it or guard it—everybody pays.

One way or another.

Death and Dignity: Handling Tragedy in Westerns

Death walks beside every character in a Western. Sometimes it's quick, loud, and public—a gunshot echoing across the street. Sometimes it's quiet, drawn out, and personal—a cough behind a closed door, a final letter folded by firelight. In a land that never promised safety, death was as common as dust. But what gives it power in your story isn't just that it happens—it's how it happens, and how the people around it live with the loss. Tragedy in a Western isn't just about who dies. It's about what that death means, how it shifts the story, and how the characters carry that weight.

You don't have to be dramatic to write tragedy well. In fact, the most devastating scenes are often the most restrained. A cowboy returning home to find the house cold and empty. A mother laying her child in the earth with no priest and no choir. A friend watching another fall, then riding on without saying a word. Westerns thrive on understatement. What's not said is just as important as what is. Use ChatGPT to explore this: *"Write a Western scene where a character quietly grieves after losing someone important."* You'll find that silence can do more than a full page of dialogue.

When someone dies in a Western, it should shift the balance of the world around them. That death should matter. Maybe it sparks revenge. Maybe it ends a feud. Maybe it opens a path for forgiveness that wouldn't have happened otherwise. Let the story ripple outward from the tragedy. Ask ChatGPT: *"Describe the consequences in a Western town after the respected sheriff dies suddenly."* The tension, the uncertainty, the fear—it doesn't have to be loud, but it should be deep.

Characters don't have to show grief the same way. One man might break down. Another might harden. One might drink himself into a stupor. Another might ride out to find the person responsible. And some won't show anything at all—because in the West, sorrow was often swallowed, not shared. Ask ChatGPT: *"Create three characters who all react differently to the same tragic death in a Western story."* Those contrasts will help you write layered, authentic reactions.

Let the land reflect the loss. A burial in the middle of nowhere. A storm rolling in as someone says goodbye. A coyote call breaking the silence after a body is lowered into the ground. The Western landscape always feels bigger than the characters—but in a moment of death, it can feel closer, almost like it's watching. Ask: *"Write a funeral scene on the prairie in a Western where nature plays a symbolic role."* The environment doesn't speak, but it mourns in its own way.

Tragedy also gives your protagonist a turning point. Maybe they're already broken, and the death pushes them over the edge. Or maybe they've been selfish and this moment forces growth. A character who loses someone important is now faced with a question: who are they without that person? What will they become now? You can prompt ChatGPT: *"Describe the emotional arc of a Western protagonist who loses their partner and must continue alone."* This isn't about plot—it's about identity, and how grief reshapes it.

Don't shy away from showing dignity in death. Even outlaws die with their boots on. Even villains can meet their end with a final word that stings. Even children face death with eyes wide open. Writing dignity into death doesn't mean making it heroic—it means giving it meaning. Let the character's final choice, final words, or final breath carry a truth that resonates. Ask ChatGPT: *"Write a Western death scene where a dying character passes wisdom to someone younger."* It's not sentimentality—it's legacy.

At the same time, some deaths are senseless. That's part of the Western truth. A bullet that finds the wrong man. A horse that stumbles. A fever that takes the strongest. These moments can be written with brutal honesty, because sometimes the world of the frontier didn't give answers. And sometimes that lack of resolution is exactly what shapes the characters left behind. Prompt: *"Write a Western scene where a character dies suddenly and another must bury them without understanding why it happened."* The pain in that moment isn't just from the loss—it's from the questions left behind.

You can also use death to show history. A graveyard filled with worn headstones. A child asking about names carved into wood. A character visiting a spot where someone died twenty years before. The past haunts the West, and death leaves deep footprints. Ask ChatGPT: *"Describe a Western setting where the presence of death lingers in the landscape."* That atmosphere becomes part of your story's soul.

And when you write death, don't forget the living. The one who has to carry the saddle home. The one who finds the note too late. The one who hears the gunshot from across the hills and knows without seeing. These reactions matter more than the death itself. They keep the grief alive in the story. They shape what comes next. Ask: *"Write the scene after a Western funeral where two characters argue about what to do next."* Grief doesn't always unify—it can divide, confuse, ignite.

Western tragedy is about more than who lives and dies. It's about *how* they lived. What they stood for. What they left behind. The hat hung on a peg. The boots by the fire. The name someone can't stop whispering. These details speak volumes. Use them.

Because death in a Western isn't just an ending.

It's a mark on the land.

A silence in the wind.

A story someone else has to finish.

Using Suspense to Keep the Reader Turning Pages

Suspense in a Western doesn't always come from bullets flying or horses galloping into town with dust at their heels. Sometimes it comes from a knock that doesn't get answered. A rider spotted on the horizon, not moving. A character reaching slowly for a gun while pretending to laugh. Suspense isn't about chaos—it's about *potential.* It's the feeling that something is about to happen, that something *could* happen, and the reader doesn't know when or how. That tension, drawn like a wire across the story, is what keeps them turning pages deep into the night.

At its core, suspense is built on *questions without answers.* Who's coming down the trail? What's in that saddlebag? Why did the sheriff suddenly go quiet when that name was mentioned? To build suspense, you don't need to overwhelm the reader with information—you need to withhold it just long enough to make them lean forward. You can use ChatGPT to help structure these moments with prompts like: *"Give me five suspense-building questions for a Western story about a missing person."* Each question becomes a door you open slowly, letting the reader peek inside, but never flinging it wide.

Suspense also thrives in the gap between what the reader knows and what the character knows. Maybe the reader saw the outlaw slip poison into the bottle, but the protagonist hasn't had a drink yet. Maybe we know a trap has been set at the pass, but the ranchers are riding straight into it. That tension—the dramatic irony—makes every line a coil waiting to spring. Ask ChatGPT: *"Describe a Western scene where the reader knows danger is ahead, but the characters do not."* That gives you pacing that crackles with dread.

Dialogue can become a powerful tool for suspense. It's not just what's said—it's what's *not* said. A man walks into a saloon and casually mentions a name that makes everyone freeze. A woman offers a stranger a place to stay but never asks who he is. A lawman interrogates a prisoner who keeps giving polite, smiling answers while blood drips from his handcuffs. The tension hides in tone, in pauses, in double meanings. Prompt ChatGPT: *"Write a tense Western conversation where both characters are lying, but neither wants to reveal it."* That kind of exchange pulls the reader in, line by line, trying to guess who will slip first.

Setting and environment can amplify suspense in quiet, powerful ways. A storm rolling in. A barn door creaking open on its own. The sound of hoofbeats echoing but no rider in sight. These aren't just atmospheric details—they're psychological tools. They signal to the reader that things are shifting, that danger might be near, or might already be here. Ask ChatGPT: *"Describe a suspenseful night scene in a Western ghost town."* With the right setting, even silence becomes threatening.

Suspense is also about pacing. Slow it down when it counts. Don't rush to the reveal. Let the character walk the hall, light the lantern, hear the floorboard creak. Let them hesitate before opening the letter. Let them sense they're being watched before they confirm it. These delays build anticipation. You can ask ChatGPT to structure the rhythm: *"Outline a suspenseful Western scene with a slow buildup to sudden violence."* Each beat pulls the reader closer to the edge.

Sometimes, suspense works best when the danger isn't obvious. Maybe the threat isn't a gunman—it's a secret. Maybe the tension isn't about who gets shot—but who's telling the truth. In a Western, suspicion is just as sharp as a blade. A stranger who won't say why he's in town. A friend who starts acting different after a visit to the bank. A preacher who locks his church doors at night. Ask: *"Create a Western plot where suspense builds around a hidden betrayal within a close-knit community."* That kind of story simmers.

Letting readers think something terrible *might* happen can be more powerful than actually making it happen. Suspense doesn't always need to pay off with violence. It might twist into a reveal, a revelation, or a reversal. The outlaw might turn out to be the law. The stolen gold might be fake. The loyal deputy might be the one who set the fire. That *twist*—that moment when the reader realizes what they thought they knew was wrong—is the payoff. Use ChatGPT to brainstorm: *"Give me five suspenseful plot twists for a Western drama."* Then seed hints and misdirections along the way to keep your readers guessing.

Character decisions drive suspense when they're placed under pressure. A rancher hiding a fugitive. A sheriff forced to choose between the law and his friend. A woman who knows the man she loves killed someone, but doesn't know why. These emotional traps make the suspense personal. They make the reader care about more than just who survives—they care about *how* the choice will change the character. Prompt ChatGPT: *"Write a Western scene where a character must decide whether to betray someone they love to save themselves."* The suspense here comes from moral gravity, not gunpowder.

And don't forget the value of *unresolved tension*. End a chapter on a question. On a breath. On a knock. Leave the reader wondering what's just out of sight. Ask: *"List suspenseful chapter endings for a Western novel."* You don't need a cliffhanger every time, but you do need momentum. A reason to keep going. A hint that the storm hasn't passed yet.

Because the West wasn't just dangerous—it was uncertain.

And suspense is the feeling of uncertainty with a heartbeat.

When done right, it's the sound of spurs outside the door... and the silence before the knock.

Writing a Poetic Western: Rhythm in Your Prose

The Western isn't just grit and gunpowder—it's poetry riding in a saddle. When done right, the prose of a Western doesn't just tell a story, it sings. Not in rhyme, necessarily, but in rhythm. In tone. In the quiet cadence of a man walking into the wind or a woman whispering to the land that refuses to love her back. Writing a poetic Western is about letting the landscape breathe, letting the silence between words say as much as the words themselves, and shaping sentences the way the wind shapes the canyon walls—slowly, naturally, and always with purpose.

Poetic prose in the Western tradition draws power from simplicity. You don't need flowery language or complex metaphors. You need clean lines with weight behind them. You need the kind of writing where every sentence feels carved out of stone, not just typed on a page. A rider approaches a town. A shot rings out in the dusk. A father buries his son. The language shouldn't shout. It should whisper with authority. You can prompt ChatGPT: *"Write a Western paragraph with poetic language and a somber tone."* You'll get a sense of how restraint becomes beauty.

Rhythm is at the heart of this style. Short. Then shorter. Then a sentence that draws out like a dusty road stretching to the horizon. Varying sentence length creates tension and relief, like the breath between gallops. You can write an entire scene with rhythm alone—how a paragraph slows as a man lays his rifle down, or speeds up as a posse gives chase. Use ChatGPT to help you experiment: *"Rewrite this Western action scene with a slow, poetic rhythm."* The pacing will shift the mood entirely.

Repetition is another poetic device that works beautifully in the Western. Repeating a phrase like "he didn't look back" or "the wind kept blowing" ties your prose to the heartbeat of the land. The frontier was repetition—of days, of losses, of footsteps in the same dry dust. That echo adds emotional weight and gives your writing the timeless quality of an old folk song. Prompt: *"Write a Western passage using repetition to create mood."* You'll feel the rhythm before you understand the meaning—and that's the mark of poetic writing.

A poetic Western often finds its soul in the land. The hills speak. The wind listens. The sky watches. This isn't fantasy—it's reverence. The terrain is alive, and your prose should treat it that way. Let the grass bend when a rider passes. Let the dust rise like a ghost behind a wagon. Ask ChatGPT: *"Describe a Western desert at dusk using poetic imagery."* That kind of writing grounds the reader not just in place, but in feeling.

Character introspection in a poetic Western isn't overdone—it's measured. A man might stare into the fire and think about the war. A woman might trace the edge of a broken locket and say nothing at all. Use interiority sparingly but with weight. One line of honest thought can crack open a chapter. Ask: *"Write a poetic internal monologue from a Western character grieving in silence."* The right words, at the right moment, are more powerful than a hundred shouted lines.

You can also use metaphor and simile, but sparingly, and only if they grow from the soil of the West itself. A man's soul might be dry as a riverbed. A woman's anger might rise like smoke from wet wood. A memory might cling like burrs on wool. These are images the reader can feel, smell, see. Ask ChatGPT: *"Give me original metaphors rooted in Western imagery."* Then use just one or two—never too many, never all at once.

Dialogue in a poetic Western can be sharp and spare. A few words, heavy with meaning. A character might say, "He ain't comin' back," and that's all. Poetic doesn't mean grand—it means *exact*. You can prompt: *"Write a poetic Western dialogue exchange between two enemies who respect each other."* The silence between their words might say more than the bullets ever could.

To maintain poetic tone across an entire chapter, consider bookending your scenes with image or mood. Start with the wind over the plains. End with a boot-print fading into the dust. That structure brings your reader full circle and gives the story an almost meditative rhythm. Ask: *"Outline a poetic Western scene with a symbolic opening and closing image."* You'll find that story becomes more than plot—it becomes experience.

A poetic Western can still have action, violence, conflict—but it handles them with reverence. Death isn't just an ending—it's a punctuation mark in the song of the land. The way someone falls, the way the sky changes, the way another character kneels beside the body—those are the lines your reader remembers. Prompt: *"Write a death scene in a poetic Western style, focusing on the land's reaction rather than gore."* That tone changes everything.

In the end, writing a poetic Western is about listening. Listening to the rhythm of horses' hooves. The hush of stars over open plains. The soft click of a revolver being loaded in the dark. Your prose becomes the wind through the canyon, not a voice shouting over it.

Because the West isn't just a place to fight or flee—it's a place to feel.

And when your story reads like a hymn to that wide, lonesome country,

the reader doesn't just turn the page—they *linger*.

And they remember.

Campfires and Conversations: Quiet Moments with Meaning

Not every moment in a Western needs a gun drawn or a horse galloping through the dust. Some of the most powerful scenes unfold in the quiet glow of a campfire, where words are chosen carefully, or not at all. A campfire is where characters take off the armor of bravado and silence and speak as people, not roles. It's where enemies might become reluctant allies, lovers might finally say what matters, or someone who hasn't spoken in pages finally opens up. These moments don't just develop character—they bind the entire story with threads of truth, regret, hope, and memory. And when written well, they can leave more impact than any gunfight ever could.

The campfire strips everything away. It's not a fancy setting. It's just open land, a little light, some warmth against the cold, and the dark pressing in all around. That simplicity creates honesty. There's no stage, no crowd, no safety net. Just people, the night, and time to think. If you're writing a Western scene where your characters are about to change, consider placing it beside a fire. Prompt ChatGPT: *"Write a Western campfire scene between two characters with unresolved tension."* You'll get something slow-burning, intimate, and ripe for emotional weight.

Dialogue by firelight works differently than in daylight. It's slower. Softer. There's a natural rhythm to it, with pauses that say more than the words themselves. A character might stare into the flames before answering. Might hesitate before sharing something painful. Might lie to protect someone, even when the truth is hovering just above the embers. Try prompting: *"Create a Western dialogue where one character tells a story to hide the truth."* In scenes like this, storytelling becomes survival.

Sometimes campfire conversations aren't even about the big things. They're about small memories that reveal character. A favorite meal from childhood. The first horse they ever rode. A superstition passed down from a mother or a song their brother used to hum. These quiet exchanges don't push the plot forward—they deepen the soul of your characters. Ask ChatGPT: *"Give me five personal memories a Western character might share during a campfire conversation."* These details can bond characters and soften them without breaking their edge.

You can also use the campfire to stage conflict—but in a quieter key. A hidden resentment. A long-held secret. A confrontation that starts as small talk. Maybe two riders haven't spoken since a man was shot back in town, and now the silence stretches too far. The fire crackles. The tension rises. One speaks. The other doesn't. These aren't explosive arguments. They're controlled burns, meant to reveal, not destroy. Try: *"Write a Western scene where two allies confront each other at a campfire over a shared past."* That tension, kept low and smoldering, pulls readers in closer.

Silence matters just as much as speech. Some characters don't say much, but their actions beside the fire speak volumes. Handing over a blanket. Sharing the last piece of jerky. Staring at the stars while someone else talks. These gestures can say what the characters can't. The fire lets people sit in silence without it feeling empty. It feels *earned.* You can prompt: *"Describe a silent Western campfire scene that shows unspoken understanding between two characters."* Sometimes the best writing in these moments isn't in the lines—it's between them.

Use the fire itself as a symbol. It's warmth, but also danger. It keeps predators away but reveals your position. It gives comfort but can vanish with one gust of wind. In a Western, the campfire becomes a metaphor for vulnerability and trust. Two characters choosing to sleep near the same flame says they believe—at least for now—that the other won't slit their throat in the night. Ask: *"What are some symbolic meanings of a campfire in Western storytelling?"* These ideas can help you infuse your scene with depth, even if nothing "happens."

Poetic prose thrives in firelight. You can slow down your narration here, let your sentences stretch, your images glow. Describe the way the sparks fly like fireflies, the way the smoke curls like a question, the way the wood snaps like bones long buried. Use rhythm to mirror the flickering flame—short bursts followed by longer, glowing lines. Prompt ChatGPT: *"Write a poetic Western paragraph set around a dying campfire."* That kind of language gives your scene lasting texture.

You can also use the campfire as a moment of decision. A character finally chooses to return home. Another admits they can't outrun what's chasing them. A third reveals they've been lying all along. The fire becomes a circle of truth, burning away the masks worn all day. Ask ChatGPT: *"Create a Western scene where a campfire conversation leads to a major decision."* The quiet before the storm is sometimes louder than the storm itself.

In screenwriting, the visual of a campfire casts everything in shadows and glow. Faces half-lit. Eyes flickering. Movements slow and deliberate. A hat pulled low. A gun cleaned in silence. Every moment here is cinematic. And it's not just a break between action scenes—it's where you let the audience *feel.* Let them sit. Let them lean in. Let them breathe before the story explodes again. Ask: *"Storyboard a Western campfire scene where tension and intimacy mix."* You'll find it becomes one of the most memorable moments in the script.

Because in the West, not all truths were shouted from rooftops.

Some were whispered beside the flames.

Some were hidden in stories told to the stars.

And some were spoken in silence, while the fire burned low and no one dared to look away.

Making the Landscape a Character in the Story

In a Western, the landscape isn't just background—it's alive. It breathes. It waits. It punishes. It protects. It shapes the people who ride across it and becomes the silent witness to their struggles. When you treat the land as a character, it begins to carry weight in every scene. It doesn't speak with words, but with storms, shadows, and wind. It doesn't move quickly, but it always moves. And like any great character, it changes the others around it. Writing a Western without giving the land a presence is like writing a war story without tension, or a love story without longing—it just doesn't work.

The Western landscape is wide, wild, and deeply unforgiving. But it's also beautiful, poetic, and filled with symbolism. The desert isn't just a dry place. It's a test. The mountains aren't just tall. They're ancient, immovable truths. The prairie isn't just grass—it's freedom, and loneliness, and danger, all at once. You can use ChatGPT to explore these concepts: *"Describe a Western desert as if it were a living character watching the story unfold."* What you'll get is atmosphere layered with emotion, history, and meaning.

The trick is to write the land with intention. Not just as a setting—but as a force. Let it challenge the protagonist. Let it hide things. Let it reveal things. A rider may think he's alone, but the buzzards know different. A woman may bury something in the ground and think it's forgotten—but the next flood brings it back. The land doesn't forget. Ask: *"Write a Western scene where the landscape thwarts a character's plan."* That gives the land a voice without dialogue.

Seasons, weather, and light play important roles too. A story set under the relentless sun feels different from one that unfolds under falling snow. Rain can cleanse or flood. Wind can carry whispers or warnings. Dusk can mean safety or signal ambush. When you're crafting scenes, think about what the land is doing as much as what the characters are doing. Ask ChatGPT: *"Describe a Western thunderstorm from the perspective of a character riding through open range."* That perspective blends mood with setting in a powerful way.

Characters should react to the land the way they react to people. With awe. With fear. With respect. A gunfighter might fear no man, but he won't cross the desert without water. A rancher might fight to keep his land not because it's valuable, but because it's the only thing that's ever been constant. Use prompts like: *"Create a Western character whose emotional state mirrors the land they live on."* That deepens both your character and your world.

Let the land hold memory. A burned-out homestead. A grave with no marker. An abandoned trail no one takes anymore because of what happened there. The past clings to the land in a Western. It can be felt even when it's not spoken. You can prompt: *"Write a Western scene where the landscape reminds a character of something they're trying to forget."* These ghostly connections give your setting emotional resonance.

And think about how different characters see the same land differently. A cattleman sees grazing land. A Native warrior sees sacred ground. A railroad baron sees progress. A widow sees the grave of her husband. The land hasn't changed—but its meaning has. That's where the storytelling deepens. Ask: *"Describe a Western valley from four different perspectives."* That contrast brings layers to your narrative without changing the physical scene at all.

Use the land to mirror the story's emotional arc. A character begins in fertile plains—safe, simple. Then comes the desert—hard, dry, unforgiving. Finally, the mountain—a climb, a challenge, an ending. If your plot has shape, let your landscape echo it. A Western is a journey, and the terrain should reflect the emotional path your characters are riding. Prompt: *"Outline a Western story where the landscape changes alongside the character's emotional growth."* The physical journey becomes a metaphor.

In visual storytelling, let the land steal the scene. A single rider crossing a salt flat. A cabin under stormy skies. The long shadow of a cactus at sundown. These images are not filler—they are *feeling*. They create space for the reader or viewer to breathe, reflect, absorb. You can ask ChatGPT: *"List iconic Western visual moments where the landscape tells the story without words."* These become your anchors for pacing and mood.

Even your action scenes can hinge on the terrain. A gunfight in the narrow walls of a canyon is very different than one in an open plain. A chase on rocky cliffs adds danger. A shootout during a dust storm becomes chaos. The land doesn't just watch the story—it participates in it. Prompt: *"Write a Western chase scene where the terrain forces a character to make a life-or-death decision."* Now the land isn't just set dressing—it's fate.

And at the end of the story, when the dust settles and the gun-smoke clears, the land remains. Maybe that's the most powerful way to show its presence. Characters die. Towns fall. Names are forgotten. But the wind still blows through the pass. The river still runs. The red rocks still hold the heat of another sunset. The land bears witness—and sometimes, it even forgives.

Because in the Western, the land doesn't just hold the story.

It is the story.

It shapes every choice, holds every memory, and waits for the next rider to leave a mark that the dust will one day carry away.

Ghost Towns, Legends, and Local Myths

Every Western town has its stories—the ones whispered after dark, told around campfires, scratched into barroom walls, or etched into half-buried gravestones. They're not always true, but that's never the point. These legends, these local myths, give soul to the setting. They explain why no one rides through the canyon at night. Why the bell in the old church still rings after midnight. Why there's a burned-out shack in the hills where children go missing if they stray too far. Writing ghost towns and folklore into your Western gives it a depth that feels older than the characters and larger than the plot. It makes your world feel like it's lived many lives before your story even begins.

A ghost town isn't just empty buildings. It's a place that remembers. Maybe the mine dried up, or the water turned bad. Maybe the railroad skipped past, and people faded like morning fog. Or maybe something darker happened—something no one talks about. You don't have to spell it out. Let the boarded-up windows, rusted signs, and half-collapsed gallows speak for themselves. Prompt ChatGPT: *"Describe an abandoned Western town with a dark history that still lingers in the air."* That setting can become a character in its own right.

These towns work best when the silence feels unnatural. When even the birds keep their distance. Maybe there's a story about a hanging gone wrong, or a preacher who cursed the ground before vanishing into the hills. These aren't just spooky details—they're layers of mystery. The ghost town is where your characters confront the past, or try to escape it. Use ChatGPT to flesh it out: *"Write a Western scene where a rider arrives in a ghost town with a reputation for being cursed."* That kind of scene walks the line between history and haunting.

Myths are born from real pain. Maybe a settler family vanished one winter and the town says it was wolves—but others say the father lost his mind. Maybe a gold strike brought dozens to a canyon, but only one man ever came back. Maybe there's a spirit said to walk the ridge, a woman in white, crying for a child no one remembers. These aren't just ghost stories—they're warnings. They say something about fear, about guilt, about what the town has tried to bury. Prompt: *"List five original Western legends that a small town might believe and pass down."* You can build an entire subplot—or an entire novel—around just one of them.

When writing these legends, don't confirm or deny them too quickly. Let your characters argue over what really happened. Let one believe, another scoff, a third refuse to talk at all. Maybe your protagonist doesn't believe in spirits—until he sees something out there no man can explain. Maybe a skeptic arrives and mocks the town's stories—until the legend reaches out and touches them. Ask ChatGPT: *"Write a conversation between two Western characters debating whether a town myth is real."* That kind of scene adds tension without a single gunshot.

You can also make myths personal. Maybe a character is connected to the story somehow. Maybe their father was the last sheriff before the town fell. Maybe their family was blamed for the town's curse. Or maybe they're unknowingly fulfilling the steps of a local prophecy. These connections deepen character and plot all at once. Try: *"Create a Western character haunted by a legend from their hometown."* Their entire motivation might grow from something that may not even be real.

And what about the people who stay behind in these ghost towns? The caretaker who's gone strange. The blind man who claims to have seen the devil. The child who hums a song no one remembers teaching them. These characters become the link between the past and the present. They're unsettling not because they say something's wrong—but because they act like it isn't. Ask: *"Describe a lone inhabitant of a Western ghost town who believes everyone else is still there."* You won't need a monster. You'll have unease by the shovelful.

Legends also affect behavior. Maybe no one builds near the old well. Maybe every saloon has a horseshoe nailed above the door—not for luck, but for protection. Maybe travelers are told not to ride after sundown through a certain pass—not by law, but by tradition. These myths become part of how people live. They don't have to believe them completely. But they don't test them either. Prompt ChatGPT: *"List local superstitions and rituals common in a Western town with a haunted reputation."* These details create atmosphere that sticks to the reader's skin.

And there's nothing wrong with leaning into the supernatural—if it fits your tone. A ghost that helps guide the protagonist. A cursed object. A forgotten grave that won't stay quiet. Just keep your story grounded in character. The myth should reflect what your characters fear, what they long for, what they regret. The best legends are metaphors made flesh. You can use ChatGPT to brainstorm: *"Create a Western ghost story that mirrors the emotional journey of the protagonist."*

Visually, ghost towns offer some of the most cinematic imagery in the genre. Bleached signs swinging in the wind. Sunlight through broken church windows. Dust drifting through the empty jail. A rider stopping in the middle of the street, hearing only the wind. These images don't need explanation—they carry weight just by existing. Prompt: *"Write a scene describing a ghost town from the perspective of someone who grew up there."* That lens turns scenery into story.

Because in the West, the dead don't always stay buried.

And a town doesn't vanish just because the map says it's gone.

The stories survive—passed from lips to firelight,

riding the wind like ash, waiting for someone brave—or foolish enough—to listen.

How to Use ChatGPT to Flesh Out Dialogue and Scenes

ChatGPT isn't just a tool for throwing ideas around—it's your writing partner that never sleeps. It won't replace your voice or vision, but it will give you the bones, the beats, and sometimes the spark you didn't know you needed. When you're writing a Western drama, especially one with weight, rhythm, and meaning, scenes and dialogue need to feel lived-in. They need dust and emotion, silence and grit. And ChatGPT can help you layer all of that in without sacrificing your creative control.

Let's start with dialogue. Western dialogue is sparse, purposeful, often poetic. It's less about what's said and more about what's implied. If you give ChatGPT a line like: *"The outlaw tells the sheriff he didn't come to fight, but his hand is already on his gun,"* and ask, *"Write the dialogue exchange between them,"* you'll get something raw and ready to shape. The result might not be your final lines—but it gives you structure. Maybe you like the cadence of a phrase. Maybe it shows you what *not* to say. Maybe it sparks something entirely new.

Dialogue also carries subtext, and ChatGPT can help you dig into it. You might say, *"Write a tense conversation between two characters who are pretending to be civil but secretly hate each other,"* and suddenly you've got a verbal duel happening without a single curse word or raised voice. In a Western, these quiet threats and polite insults are often more powerful than gunfire. You can then trim, reshape, and rewrite in your own style. The AI gives you the stone—you carve the statue.

Want to write character-specific voices? Feed ChatGPT a character sketch and ask, *"What kind of speech patterns would this character have in an 1880s Western setting?"* It will return suggestions that reflect background, region, class, and temperament. A ranch hand might drop his g's and talk in plain terms. A former preacher might use biblical turns of phrase. A gambler might sound smooth and too sure of himself. Once you know the voice, ask for sample lines. Or go scene by scene and ask: *"Write dialogue for a saloon scene between a cynical rancher and a silver-tongued banker trying to buy his land."* You'll get the rhythm of their conflict right away.

Now, when it comes to fleshing out full scenes, ChatGPT can be used in a dozen smart ways. Say you've got a rough idea: "Two riders camp for the night and finally talk about the man they buried that morning." You can prompt: *"Write a Western scene at a campfire where two riders, after burying a friend, reflect on his past and their next move."* The draft that comes back might have atmosphere, emotional tension, and character introspection. It's up to you to keep what works and sharpen the rest.

Maybe you've already written the scene and it feels flat. You can ask: *"Improve this dialogue so that it has more emotional tension and natural rhythm,"* then paste in what you've written. ChatGPT won't just clean it up—it'll offer alternative lines and phrasing. You don't have to accept the changes. But often, just seeing the rewrite helps you understand why the original didn't land.

Stuck on how to start a scene? Ask: *"Give me five ways to open a Western saloon scene that suggest rising tension,"* or *"How can I introduce a new character in a town full of people who don't trust strangers?"* The ideas that follow are often just the kick you need to get rolling again.

Scenes also benefit from sensory detail, and ChatGPT can fill that in fast. You've written "They walked into the old barn"—simple, clean. But you want to set the mood. Ask: *"Describe an old Western barn at dusk that feels like it's hiding something."* You'll get smells, sounds, shadows, and textures. You don't have to use every word, but suddenly, you've got atmosphere.

Need help with pacing? If a scene feels rushed or too slow, explain the issue and ask: *"How can I restructure this Western dialogue-heavy scene to increase dramatic tension?"* The AI might suggest rearranging lines, adding pauses, shifting the emotional arc, or creating a beat of silence before the most important line lands.

Action scenes, too, can be built step by step. A simple prompt like: *"Write a Western shootout between a lone rider and two bounty hunters in an alley behind a saloon,"* will return a full sequence. You can take that draft and revise it to match your tone, add your character's internal thoughts, or strip it back to match the poetic realism of your world.

You can also use ChatGPT for building in symbolism. Ask: *"Suggest symbolic imagery for a Western scene where a man buries his past,"* and it might return ideas like a dying fire, a rusted horseshoe, a broken mirror in the saddlebag. You pick the ones that fit. You use them as anchors for your scene.

Working on rewrites? Paste your original and ask: *"How can I rewrite this scene to feel more emotionally charged without adding extra dialogue?"* ChatGPT might recommend moments of body language, interiority, or setting contrast that intensify what's already there. This kind of feedback keeps you from overwriting and losing that Western restraint.

And most importantly, you stay in charge. ChatGPT doesn't write *for* you. It writes *with* you. It builds from your ideas, your themes, your rhythms. It doesn't know your characters like you do, but it helps you explore them from every angle. It gives you options, variations, and structure when you're too deep in the story to see the way out.

So whether you're stuck in the mud or riding full speed and just need a hand wrangling what's ahead, let ChatGPT be the partner who never asks for credit.

It holds the lantern when the trail gets dark.

It hands you a line when your character falls silent.

And it helps you turn firelight and footsteps into something that breathes on the page.

From Prompt to Plot Twist: Letting AI Guide the Ride

One of the most exciting things about using ChatGPT to write a Western drama is not just its ability to generate content—it's the unexpected detours it can take you on. You might start with a simple idea about a rider returning home, and before you know it, you're unraveling a lost identity, a buried secret, or a betrayal no one saw coming. This is where ChatGPT truly shines—not by replacing creativity, but by jolting it into motion. When you know how to feed it the right prompts and let go of the reins just enough, it can lead you straight to a twist that gives your story the weight it was missing.

Let's say you start with a prompt like: *"A bounty hunter rides into town to collect a reward, but something feels off."* That's your seed. A straightforward setup. But now ask ChatGPT: *"What five plot twists could happen in this story that shift the perspective of who the bounty hunter really is?"* Suddenly you're handed variations where the hunter is actually the hunted, or where the bounty never existed at all, or where the bounty was set by someone close to him for reasons he doesn't yet know. With just one follow-up, your straight road has turned into a maze of intriguing possibilities.

The beauty of AI-guided storytelling is that you don't have to commit right away. You explore. You test. You prompt variations. Think of it like scouting the land before building the town. You can try: *"What if the man who posted the bounty is the real villain?"* or *"Give me a scene where the bounty turns out to be the hunter's own brother."* Each twist can be run through the machine, refined, explored from different character angles. You keep what sings, toss what doesn't, and build from the sparks.

AI works best when you get specific. The prompt *"Give me a twist"* is too broad. But *"Give me a betrayal twist that would make a hardened gunslinger question everything he believes about justice"* will return a moment with emotional gravity. ChatGPT starts to become not just a brainstorming tool, but a lens that zooms in on the emotional truth of your story. That's what a great plot twist should do—not just surprise, but *clarify*. It should force your character to change, or admit something they've avoided.

Let's take a quiet scene, like two characters watching the fire die. You might say: *"They've been friends for years. One of them is hiding something terrible. What are five things that could come out in this moment that would reframe their relationship?"* From there, you get twists that change direction. Maybe one of them caused the death they've both been mourning. Maybe one was never who they claimed to be. Maybe the friendship was built on a lie that's finally cracking. You follow whichever path stirs your gut—and write toward the emotional fallout.

The key is letting the twist grow from character and theme—not just from shock value. If your Western is about redemption, make the twist challenge the idea of whether a man can truly change. If it's about justice, twist the perception of guilt and innocence. Prompt: *"What's a character-based twist in a Western that challenges the meaning of redemption?"* The result will feel earned, not gimmicky.

Don't be afraid to chase unexpected suggestions. Sometimes ChatGPT will throw something out of left field—like a preacher who used to be an outlaw, or a gold mine that was never real. You might not use that exact idea, but it can lead you somewhere stronger. Maybe the preacher's lie was to protect someone. Maybe the fake gold mine was planted to drive people away from something worse. One twist becomes the soil for another.

Twists also work better when seeded early, and ChatGPT can help you plant them. Ask: *"What are subtle clues I can plant in the first three chapters that hint at a plot twist where the town doctor is the villain?"* The returned details—odd behavior, things left unsaid, mismatched stories—give you building blocks to make your twist land hard without feeling cheap.

You can also reverse engineer the twist. Start with it and work backwards. Let's say your endgame is: *"The sheriff faked his own death and has been controlling the town in secret."* Ask ChatGPT: *"How would this twist affect earlier scenes without giving it away too soon?"* This process lets you weave in breadcrumbs—enough for readers to look back and go, "Of course," without ever seeing it coming.

Twists aren't just for endings. You can plant them mid-story to rewire the narrative. Maybe the man your protagonist is hunting is actually the only person who can save him. Maybe the outlaw he's chasing is the only witness to a crime he himself committed. Ask: *"What twist could force a hero to team up with his worst enemy in a Western drama?"* These turning points shift the emotional and moral stakes, and keep the reader flipping pages.

You can also test multiple twists. Use the same scene and rewrite it three different ways. Ask:

"Write this scene with a betrayal twist."

"Now rewrite it with a supernatural twist."

"Now with a personal revelation twist."

Compare them. See which one opens the story wider. See which one speaks to your theme. Keep following the thread that pulls at you.

Because a Western isn't just about the trail—it's about the fork in the road.

The moment where everything turns.

Where the person you trusted isn't who you thought.

Where the truth was waiting in the dust all along.

And with ChatGPT, the twist is always within reach.

All you have to do is ask the right question

—and be brave enough to ride where it leads.

Drawing Maps of the Mind: Using Psychology to Motivate

Western characters are built from the land, but they're shaped by the roads they've ridden in their minds. The dust and blood on their boots might tell the surface story, but the real narrative—the one that matters—is happening inside them. A hardened lawman who doesn't sleep. A gunslinger who won't talk about the war. A widow who stares at the horizon as if it owes her something. These aren't just personalities—they're psychological blueprints. And when you write a Western with psychology in your holster, every choice becomes deeper, every twist more believable, and every showdown twice as powerful.

To write motivated, complex characters, you've got to look beneath the hat and badge. You've got to ask: *What does this character truly want?* Not just money, land, or revenge. What do they *need*? Safety? Control? Forgiveness? Recognition? Freedom? Love? Once you know that, the plot becomes a reflection of that need—twisted, tested, and ultimately transformed. You can start with a prompt like: *"Create a Western character whose motivation is rooted in abandonment."* From there, their behavior takes on layers. They might fear connection. Or chase validation. Or destroy anything that feels like home before it can leave them.

Fear is one of the most powerful motivators in a Western. Fear of being weak. Fear of dying in obscurity. Fear of not measuring up to a father's legacy. These fears drive men to pick up guns, ride into storms, or destroy what they love most. Ask ChatGPT: *"What hidden fear could drive a Western sheriff to become increasingly violent?"* The answers might be surprising—fear of change, fear of being irrelevant, fear of being seen for who he really is.

Trauma is another deep well for motivation. The Western is a genre that thrives on history—both personal and collective. The Civil War. Family massacres. Betrayals on the trail. These aren't just backstory—they're living things, echoing in the minds of your characters. A man who lost his entire cavalry unit might avoid conflict but erupt in moments of stress. A woman who buried her husband might be fiercely independent but quick to push people away. Prompt: *"Describe a Western protagonist whose trauma informs their decisions but who refuses to speak about it."* That silence becomes its own kind of voice.

Another key aspect of motivation is *belief systems*. A character may act out of moral codes, religious views, cultural traditions, or twisted philosophies. A bounty hunter might believe that redemption is earned through blood. A preacher might see every act of violence as God's will. A rancher might believe that loyalty means never turning on family, no matter what they've done. Ask ChatGPT: *"Create three contrasting belief systems for characters in a Western, each shaping how they interpret justice."* This gives your story internal tension even before the plot unfolds.

Psychological tension also thrives in contradictions. A character might be outwardly brave but internally plagued with self-doubt. A pacifist might keep a revolver in their boot. A drunk might be the wisest man in the room. These contradictions make people *real*. And when those contradictions clash—internally or with others—you get drama that sticks. Ask ChatGPT: *"Write a Western character profile built on emotional contradictions."* The character might emerge broken, fascinating, and perfectly suited for the West.

Motivations should also evolve. A character might begin with the desire for revenge but discover they actually crave peace. Or they might believe they're protecting someone when, deep down, they're trying to fix a mistake they made years ago. These shifts happen in key scenes—when the character fails, when they lose someone, when they see themselves clearly for the first time. Ask: *"Describe an emotional turning point in a Western where a character's motivation is revealed to be something else entirely."* That moment can change the entire tone of your story.

You can also chart your characters' emotional landscapes. Use a simple map: Where are they now emotionally? What scars do they carry? What are they afraid to admit? What lie do they tell themselves? What truth are they afraid of? Prompt ChatGPT with: *"Help me chart a psychological arc for a Western hero haunted by a decision he made in the war."* The map that unfolds won't be linear—but neither are human hearts.

Characters don't exist in isolation. Relationships press on their psyches. A hardened gunman might soften around a child, but not show it. A widow might lash out at kindness because it reminds her of what she's lost. A deputy might blindly follow orders from a sheriff because he never learned to trust his own judgment. These dynamics create psychological friction. Ask ChatGPT: *"Describe how a Western protagonist's internal conflict causes tension with their closest ally."* That tension is what makes scenes sing.

Even your antagonist should be psychologically sound. No one is evil for the sake of it—not in a Western that aims for depth. Maybe the outlaw's cruelty comes from years of abuse. Maybe the land baron is obsessed with control because he watched his family lose everything. Prompt: *"Write a Western villain motivated by a fear of chaos and loss."* You'll find their cruelty becomes heartbreaking—and far more dangerous.

And if you ever get stuck, reverse-engineer motivation. Take a big moment—say, a character shoots someone in cold blood—and ask *why*. Was it revenge? Panic? Did they see their father in that man's face? Did they believe they were saving someone? Keep asking *why* until you hit bedrock. That's where the truth lives. That's where you find the scene's soul.

Because in a Western, the gun is just a tool.

The land is just a stage.

The real story—the lasting story—is what's going on behind the eyes.

The broken compass of a wounded soul.

The map of the mind that leads to redemption... or ruin.

The Drifter's Journey: Isolation, Purpose, and Fate

The drifter is one of the most iconic figures in all of Western storytelling. He appears on the horizon, alone, dust-covered, unknown. No one knows where he came from, and no one knows where he's going. He doesn't stay. He doesn't belong. He's a stranger to the town, a ghost to the past, and a question mark to the future. And yet, the drifter's presence always shifts something. Something in the town, something in the people, and—if the story is told right—something in himself. Writing the drifter's journey is less about what he does and more about *why he does it*. It's a study of isolation, the slow uncovering of purpose, and the magnetic pull of fate.

To write a powerful drifter character, you have to start with the silence. The absence. The deliberate distance he keeps from everyone and everything. This man doesn't explain himself. He doesn't volunteer information. He walks into the saloon, orders something simple, scans the room, and says little. But even in that silence, he's building a story. Prompt ChatGPT: *"Describe a Western drifter through the eyes of a bartender who doesn't trust him."* What you'll get isn't just appearance—it's presence. That hard-to-name sense that this man has seen things, lost things, maybe done things he regrets.

The drifter is a man unmoored from the world. He has no home, no title, and often no name people remember. This detachment makes him feel timeless. He could be from anywhere. He might carry scars from war, from betrayal, from the simple weight of survival. Ask: *"Write a monologue from a Western drifter explaining why he doesn't stay in one place."* That interior truth, even if never spoken aloud in your story, gives you a spine to write from.

Despite—or maybe because of—his isolation, the drifter always finds himself pulled into the affairs of others. A corrupt sheriff. A threatened widow. A child in trouble. A town rotting from the inside. And he never asks to get involved. But he does. Why? Because under that silence, under that coat and dust, there is a code. The drifter doesn't talk about it, but he lives by it. Maybe it's justice. Maybe it's redemption. Maybe it's just a quiet refusal to let evil win. Prompt ChatGPT: *"Create a code of ethics for a silent Western drifter who helps people but avoids praise."* That code becomes the compass that guides him, even if he's never the one to speak it aloud.

The beauty of the drifter's arc is that it can begin in aimlessness. He rides not toward something, but *away* from it. Maybe it's guilt. Maybe it's grief. Maybe he lost someone or something he can't face. That past—whatever it is—rides with him like a shadow. It doesn't need to be revealed all at once. Let it surface in glimpses: a reaction to a name. A refusal to cross a certain river. A nightmare. A scar. You can ask: *"Write a Western scene where the drifter hears something that triggers a memory from a life he's left behind."* That fracture becomes the first crack in his armor.

What makes the drifter story emotionally rich is the slow shift from detachment to meaning. A character who thought he had no place in the world begins to *care*. He doesn't say it. But he starts checking on the townsfolk. He steps in when the kid is bullied. He fixes a fence that wasn't his to fix. And eventually, he stands between the innocent and danger. Not because he was asked—but because he *chooses* to. That moment—that *choice*—is the axis of the drifter's journey. Ask ChatGPT: *"Describe a turning point in a Western story where a drifter chooses to fight for something he never intended to care about."* That decision redefines him.

Fate plays a subtle but vital role in the drifter's tale. He never meant to stop in this town. He never meant to meet *her*. He never meant to hear *that name*. But the West has a way of pulling people toward what they're running from. Fate isn't always a grand, supernatural thing in a Western—it's a coincidence that's too perfect. A wrong turn that leads exactly where it needs to. A horse going lame at just the right—or wrong—moment. Prompt: *"Create a sequence where a Western drifter's random arrival sets off a chain of events that feels like fate."* Let the world move around him in ways he can't control. Let the story feel bigger than his choices, even as his choices matter deeply.

The end of the drifter's arc is always bittersweet. He doesn't settle down, even if people want him to. He doesn't take credit, even if he deserves it. He rarely stays. But he leaves something behind—a safer town, a changed person, a memory. And maybe—just maybe—he carries something new with him. A little less pain. A little more peace. Or a reason to ride toward something, instead of away from it. Ask ChatGPT: *"Write the final thoughts of a Western drifter as he leaves a town he helped save."* That exit, quiet and uncelebrated, becomes one of the most emotionally powerful moments in any Western.

The drifter isn't the loudest character in your story, but he is often the heart. He's the figure who shows us what it means to act without promise of reward. To protect without belonging. To keep riding, even when the road runs out. His strength is in his solitude, but his growth is in the moments when he breaks it. When he connects. When he stands for something.

Because the drifter's journey is the journey of everyone who's ever felt alone.

Everyone who's run from something and found themselves walking straight back into it.

Everyone who thinks they have no place—until they make one by what they choose to do.

He rides out before the sun is up.

And no one may ever know his name.

But what he leaves behind—

That's the part that stays.

Love and Loss in a Harsh World

In the Western, love rarely comes easy—and it almost never lasts without scars. It isn't dressed in fancy words or serenaded with violins. It rides hard, survives droughts, waits out wars, and sometimes dies quietly in the dust. Love in a harsh world is a fragile flame carried through a storm. That's why it matters so much when it's written well. It becomes the one thing more dangerous than a bullet and more valuable than gold. It gives characters something to protect, something to lose, and sometimes, something they'd kill for—or die for. Writing love and loss into your Western isn't about sentimentality. It's about truth. And the truth is that in the frontier, both can come in the same breath.

Start by understanding that love in a Western isn't always declared—it's shown. A man might build a corral in silence. A woman might stay up all night tending to a wound. A glance might carry more weight than a speech. These characters don't talk about their feelings much. They act. And sometimes, they act too late. You can prompt ChatGPT with: *"Write a Western scene where two characters show love without saying the word."* The moment that comes back might be quiet, but it will ring with something deeper than dialogue.

Often, Western love stories are born from survival. A widow and a ranch hand bond while defending the homestead. A doctor and a wounded outlaw fall into something real while hiding from the law. A saloon singer and a bounty hunter share one night before fate pulls them apart. These are loves that form in the cracks—between violence and silence, between sunrise and death. Ask: *"Describe a Western romance built on shared danger and mutual respect."* It's the kind of connection that feels believable, earned, and fleeting all at once.

Because in this world, love always walks with loss. That's the rule of the land. Maybe he comes home to find her gone. Maybe she waits for a letter that never arrives. Maybe they choose to walk away before the world takes one of them first. Loss gives love weight. It makes every kiss feel urgent. Every hand held feel temporary. Every goodbye feel like the last. You can prompt: *"Write a Western farewell between lovers who know they'll never see each other again."* That kind of heartbreak hits harder when it's inevitable, not dramatic.

Loss also shapes characters long after the moment has passed. A cowboy who doesn't speak much might still carry a ribbon in his saddlebag. A woman who never remarried might still walk the fence line at dusk, where he used to wait. The past clings in these stories like dust on boots. Let it linger in the way they move, the things they avoid, the stories they won't tell. Ask ChatGPT: *"Create a Western character shaped by the memory of a lost love."* That love becomes a ghost that rides with them—and sometimes, drives them.

Love isn't always romantic. In a Western, it's often found in small, fierce ways. A mother protecting her son. A man risking his life for a brother. A friend who rides through hell because of a promise made long ago. These forms of love are just as strong, and their loss can be just as devastating. You can ask: *"Write a Western scene where a character sacrifices everything for someone they love, without regret."* That kind of devotion burns into the bones of a story.

Sometimes love doesn't survive the world—but it changes the people who felt it. A loner who lets someone in, even for a while, might never go back to who he was. A woman who loses the man she loved might still fight harder because of the fire he left behind. This is where love becomes legacy—not through wedding rings, but through grit and memory and the way someone stands a little straighter because of who once walked beside them.

The Western setting tests love constantly. The law doesn't protect it. The land doesn't care about it. The people around it often don't believe in it. That's what makes it matter. If you can show two characters finding something tender in all that roughness, you've created something more powerful than any shootout. Try: *"Write a Western scene where two hardened characters admit, in their own guarded ways, that they need each other."* You'll get something jagged and beautiful, like broken glass catching the light.

And of course, sometimes the world doesn't let love live. But it never means it didn't matter. The outlaw might die before he gets back to her. The rancher might make the choice to leave so she'll be safer. The love might only last a few pages—but it changes everything. Ask ChatGPT: *"Write the inner monologue of a Western character mourning someone they loved but had to let go."* That kind of sorrow doesn't just deepen the character—it deepens the reader's investment.

The trick is to never make love feel easy. In the Western, love is labor. It's earned moment by moment. A stolen hour here, a glance across a campfire there. It's buried under guilt, hidden behind pride, and often arrives too late. But when it shows up—when it breaks through—it should feel like the only thing worth fighting for.

Because love in the West is the soft word in the hard world.

The warm hand in the cold night.

The one thing that makes staying worth it—and losing unbearable.

And when it's written with care, even loss doesn't undo it.

It just leaves a mark.

And in the West, some marks never fade.

Turning Tropes on Their Head with a Click

Western dramas are built on tradition. The lone gunslinger, the corrupt sheriff, the dusty duel at high noon—these tropes are the backbone of the genre. But if you use them the same way every time, they go stale fast. That's where the fun—and the power—of turning tropes on their head comes in. You take what the reader expects and give them something they didn't see coming. And when you're using ChatGPT as your creative tool, flipping tropes becomes as easy as asking the right question and following the trail wherever it leads.

First, let's get something straight. Tropes aren't bad. Tropes are patterns that exist because they *work*. The audience knows them, trusts them, and leans into them. But the second they can predict every move, the tension dies. So you take the trope, keep its structure, and change its outcome, purpose, or point of view. Instead of abandoning tropes, you use them like bait—and then you switch the hook. You can start simple. Ask ChatGPT: *"List ten common Western tropes."* You'll get everything from "the outlaw with a heart of gold" to "the town under siege by a land baron."

Now take one and flip it. Say you've got "the mysterious drifter who saves the town." What if he arrives and makes things worse? What if he's the villain in disguise? What if he saves the town, then tries to take it over? Prompt: *"What are five ways to subvert the 'mysterious drifter' trope in a Western story?"* Suddenly, the character you thought was the hero becomes the source of conflict—and readers stay hooked.

Maybe you want to mess with the "sheriff as the moral center" trope. That one's ripe for reinvention. What if the sheriff starts out as a good man but slowly loses his soul trying to maintain order? What if the sheriff is respected but quietly running the town like a mob boss? What if he's an imposter altogether—just wearing the badge because the last one disappeared? Ask ChatGPT: *"Write a Western scene where the respected sheriff is revealed to be the antagonist."* That reversal doesn't just surprise the reader—it forces every other character to rethink their alliances.

Tropes are especially fun to twist when you swap perspectives. A classic Western might paint a group as outlaws—but what if you tell the story from *their* side? What if the so-called bandits are protecting sacred land? What if the bounty hunter chasing them is the real villain? Prompt: *"Describe a Western story from the perspective of a group being hunted as criminals, who are actually innocent."* The genre shifts from revenge to survival, and the reader sees the West through new eyes.

You can also upend romantic tropes. The usual tale: a rugged man protects a vulnerable woman and they fall in love. What if it's the opposite? What if she's the one who rescues him, teaches him how to survive, and walks away when he's finally strong enough to stand alone? Or maybe they never fall in love at all—maybe the respect between them is deeper than romance. Ask: *"Write a Western relationship where two characters care deeply for each other but never become lovers."* That subtle inversion gives you nuance where the genre usually leans predictable.

Don't forget about settings. The Western town, the saloon, the open range—these are all familiar. Now take one and make it unfamiliar. A saloon that doubles as a church. A town with no sheriff because the people run it collectively. A dusty trail that leads into a ghost town built for a trap. Prompt: *"Describe a unique Western town that plays against classic tropes."* When the setting changes, everything else gets thrown off balance—and that's a good thing.

Gender roles are one of the richest veins for trope-twisting. The genre traditionally leans male, with women in supporting roles. Flip it. Make the lawman a woman—hardened, just, and haunted. Make the gunslinger a former schoolteacher. Make the widow the one out for revenge, with a rifle across her lap and no intention of forgiving anything. Ask ChatGPT: *"Give me five unconventional female protagonists for a Western drama."* These characters break the mold and bring modern weight to classic stories.

Tropes around violence can also be twisted. The Western often treats violence as justice. The duel. The hanging. The ambush. But what if your protagonist refuses to kill? What if they're trying to redeem themselves for a violent past, and every act of bloodshed feels like a failure, not a win? Prompt: *"Create a Western hero who has vowed never to kill again, even when the world pushes him to."* This moral conflict adds gravity where most Westerns just add bodies.

Even the "big twist" endings can be subverted. Normally, you expect the showdown. The last man standing. The revenge completed. But what if the ending is quiet? The revenge doesn't happen. The enemy rides away. The hero walks into the wilderness and chooses peace. Ask: *"Write a Western ending that avoids violence but still delivers emotional closure."* That kind of restraint can leave a deeper impression than a hundred spent bullets.

And here's the best part about doing all this with ChatGPT—it lets you *see* the twist before you write it. You can test ideas instantly. Ask:

"How can I flip the 'gold rush' trope so that the treasure is actually a curse?"

"What if the town under siege is hiding a darker secret than the attackers?"

"What's a version of the 'mentor trains a young gunfighter' story where the mentor is completely untrustworthy?"

Each of these flips creates a ripple effect that touches every part of the story. Characters grow differently. Conflict escalates differently. The reader stays unsure—engaged, questioning, curious. And that's what you want.

Because a great Western doesn't just ride the same old trail.

It cuts through new terrain.

It nods to the past, then walks the other way.

And with just one smart prompt, you can turn the familiar into something unforgettable—with a click.

Final Showdowns and Closing the Loop

The final showdown is the heart of the Western climax. It's the moment everything has been leading toward—the confrontation between justice and corruption, peace and violence, memory and vengeance. But more than a shootout or a standoff, the final showdown is a reckoning. It isn't just about who draws first. It's about who's right, who's ready, and who's changed. And if you're writing a Western drama, the key to making your final moments matter isn't just making them loud—it's making them *earned*. You've got to close the loop. Tie the end back to the beginning. Let your character face the thing they've been riding toward all along.

Start by asking what the showdown *means* to your protagonist. This isn't just about defeating the antagonist—it's about resolving something personal. Maybe they're confronting the man who killed their brother. Maybe they're facing down a former friend. Maybe they're standing between their past and the life they finally want. A great showdown is symbolic as much as it is physical. You can prompt ChatGPT: *"Describe a Western final showdown that forces the hero to confront his greatest fear."* That kind of conflict will carry emotional weight far beyond the bullets.

The tone of the showdown should reflect the journey your character has taken. If the story has been grim and slow-burning, the final confrontation should feel heavy, almost quiet. If the story's been a powder keg building tension, then maybe the showdown explodes in a few heartbeats. Either way, the pacing must feel deliberate. Don't rush it. Let the characters stare each other down. Let them speak their truth, even if it's just in a look. Prompt: *"Write a Western standoff scene that balances action with emotional closure."* The stakes here aren't just survival—they're meaning.

Location matters. Where the showdown happens says as much as what's said. Maybe it takes place in the very town where the story started. Maybe it's on the land the protagonist was trying to protect. Maybe it's in the desert, stripped of everything but the sky and the weight of decision. Ask ChatGPT: *"Give me five symbolic Western settings for a final showdown and explain their thematic meaning."* A showdown in a graveyard speaks to the past. One at a river crossing speaks to change. One in the middle of a burning field speaks to rebirth—or ruin.

Closing the loop means you bring the story full circle. If your character began as a man running from something, the ending forces him to stop running. If he started seeking vengeance, the final scene asks whether he'll take it—or walk away. If she's been hiding her past, now it catches up with her. Use callbacks from early in the story—an object, a phrase, a promise. Prompt ChatGPT: *"Write a Western ending that echoes a line of dialogue from the first chapter for emotional closure."* That symmetry gives your story resonance.

Think beyond just who lives and who dies. Ask: *What does this moment change?* Maybe the hero loses but breaks the cycle of violence. Maybe the villain wins, but the town rises up after. Maybe no one walks away, but the truth finally gets told. The outcome should reflect the story's theme. Ask ChatGPT: *"Write a Western final scene that resolves the moral conflict, not just the physical one."* Readers want the fight—but they want the meaning behind it even more.

Don't be afraid to show hesitation. A trembling hand. A missed shot. A character who doesn't want to kill anymore, but knows they might have to. These moments humanize your showdown. It's not about who's fastest—it's about who's willing to pay the price. Prompt: *"Describe a Western duel where both characters are reluctant to draw, but feel like they have no choice."* That standoff becomes a tragedy, not just a climax.

After the final shot is fired, take your time with the dust settling. Who's left standing? What do they do next? Does the town react? Does the wind return to the silence? Let that final beat breathe. Don't rush to credits or the last page. Let the reader feel the weight of what just happened. Ask ChatGPT: *"Write the closing paragraph of a Western where the hero survives the final fight but loses what they were fighting for."* That kind of ending will linger long after the book is closed.

And not every final showdown has to be a gunfight. It can be a truth revealed. A decision made. A man walking away instead of pulling the trigger. Some of the most powerful endings come not from violence, but from *refusal.* From restraint. From choosing peace in a world built on war. Prompt: *"Write a Western ending where the character breaks the cycle of violence by walking away from revenge."* That moment might feel quiet, but it will roar in the reader's heart.

Because a final showdown isn't just the end of the plot.

It's the end of the journey.

The test of who the character has become.

The moment where silence holds more truth than a thousand bullets.

And when you close the loop right, the West doesn't just ride off into the sunset.

It *echoes.*

Rewriting with ChatGPT: Polish, Refine, Repeat

Writing the first draft of your Western drama is like staking a claim—you find the land, you dig in, you get something started. But rewriting? That's where you build the house, shape the story, and strike gold. It's where you make the story *real.* And if you've got ChatGPT as your rewriting partner, you've got a tool that can help you sharpen dialogue, tighten structure, deepen character arcs, and polish prose—all without ever taking the wheel from you. This chapter is all about learning how to use AI to refine your story, sentence by sentence, idea by idea, until it sings.

The first step is knowing what you want to fix. Are your scenes too long? Is the dialogue too flat? Is the pacing off? You don't need to solve everything at once. Start small. Take a scene you've written and ask ChatGPT: *"How can I make this Western campfire scene more emotionally resonant?"* Or *"Rewrite this dialogue to sound more like a gritty 1880s cowboy."* You're not replacing your voice—you're challenging it, questioning it, giving it another layer to build from.

Let's say you've written a chapter that feels functional but not compelling. You can paste it into ChatGPT and prompt: *"Can you rewrite this Western scene to increase tension and use more vivid sensory detail?"* The AI might return a version that adds atmosphere, sharpens the beats, and gives you better pacing. You don't have to keep every word, but you'll see what works and what doesn't. Rewriting is often about seeing your own words from a new angle.

Dialogue is one of the fastest ways to upgrade your draft. If a scene feels flat, it's often because characters are saying too much or not enough. Ask: *"Can you rewrite this conversation to reveal more about the characters' relationship through subtext?"* Or *"Make this saloon standoff more intense with sharper dialogue."* The result might give you cleaner lines, stronger voices, or unexpected ways for characters to spar verbally without spelling everything out.

Sometimes a paragraph just doesn't land. Maybe it's a description of a landscape or a moment of internal reflection. It's got the right *idea,* but the rhythm's off or the word choice doesn't quite hit. Try: *"Can you rewrite this paragraph using a more poetic, Western-inspired tone?"* The revised version might give your prose a pulse, a cadence that fits the grit and grace of the frontier. You can take what works, mix it with your own language, and elevate the whole passage.

One of the most underrated uses of ChatGPT in the rewriting stage is *condensation.* Sometimes you write three paragraphs that could say the same thing in one. Ask: *"Can you rewrite this scene in half the word count without losing the mood or meaning?"* It teaches you where the fat is, how to trim without cutting heart, and how to let your words do more with less.

Rewriting isn't just about sentences—it's about structure too. Maybe you're not sure if the sequence of scenes works. Maybe the turning point comes too early or too late. Ask ChatGPT: *"Does this scene serve the protagonist's emotional arc?"* Or *"What would happen if I moved this confrontation to earlier in the story?"* ChatGPT can help you simulate that change, give you a mock-up of the result, and let you see how pacing and stakes shift.

You can also use it for theme refinement. Maybe your story is about redemption, but that theme isn't shining through. Ask: *"How can I reinforce the theme of redemption in this chapter without making it too obvious?"* ChatGPT might suggest lines, character decisions, or symbolic moments that support your theme subtly and powerfully.

Character consistency is another rewriting challenge where AI can lend a hand. If your protagonist feels different in Chapter 1 than in Chapter 6 and not by design, you can ask: *"Does this character sound consistent with their voice from earlier chapters?"* Or *"How can I show the emotional change this character has gone through without using exposition?"* You'll get notes on behavior, tone, and internal monologue to help your rewrite feel cohesive.

You can also do what I call *layered rewriting*. That means you pass the same scene through multiple filters. First for dialogue. Then for mood. Then for clarity. Then for theme. One pass at a time. With ChatGPT, that's easy. You simply re-feed the same section with a new prompt each round. You're slowly polishing the stone until it shines like a silver spur.

Even your final polishing stage benefits from AI. Ask: *"Can you go through this chapter and make the language tighter, more vivid, and more Western in style?"* Or *"Highlight any passive voice or weak transitions in this section."* What you get back isn't a replacement—it's a mirror, showing you the places that could sing louder.

And here's something important: rewriting with ChatGPT isn't about "fixing" what's broken. It's about *leveling up* what's already working. It's about taking the raw energy of your first draft and shaping it into something leaner, sharper, truer. AI can't write your story for you—but it can be the forge you use to heat and hammer your words into steel.

So write bold. Write rough. Spill it all onto the page.

Then step back, call in your AI sidekick, and ask the questions that lead you deeper.

Polish. Refine. Repeat.

Until the dust settles, the words ring true,

and your Western story stands tall—

like a lone rider on the ridge, unmistakable and unforgettable.

Keeping It Authentic While Staying Original

Western stories carry a long shadow. They come with dust in the corners, weathered faces, slow-draw standoffs, and a certain rhythm that feels like old leather boots against wood. When you write a Western drama, you're stepping into a genre soaked in tradition. But that doesn't mean you're stuck copying the past. The trick is to keep your world authentic—true to its time, voice, and grit—while making your story original, unexpected, and very much your own. It's about honoring the legacy without becoming a museum piece. And with the help of ChatGPT, you can walk that line with precision.

Authenticity starts with the *feel* of the world. The language, the weather, the way people move and speak. You want your Western to smell like whiskey and gunpowder, to echo with wagon wheels and coyote howls. But at the same time, you don't want to just recycle stock characters or familiar plots. You want to write a saloon we haven't seen before. A gunslinger we haven't met. A town that hides something no map shows. So how do you balance the grit of realism with the spark of invention?

First, know your world well enough to bend it. Use ChatGPT to explore specific details that give your setting weight: *"Describe a small cattle town in New Mexico in 1883,"* or *"What would a general store carry in a Western frontier settlement?"* The answers you get are anchors—little truths that keep the reader grounded. Once you've got those, *that's* when you start weaving your originality through them.

Let's say your story takes place in a railroad town. Authenticity means getting the lingo, the labor, the layout of the town right. But originality might mean your main character is a half-blind telegraph operator with a secret past. The details are rooted in research. The character is rooted in imagination. That's the balance. Prompt ChatGPT with: *"Create an unusual Western protagonist who lives in a historically accurate 1870s rail town."* You'll get something that blends fact and fiction in just the right measure.

When writing dialogue, authenticity means capturing the rhythm of the time without falling into parody. Don't turn every character into a cowboy cliché. One might speak plainly. Another might be poetic. Another might mix two languages. Ask: *"Write a natural-sounding conversation between a Mexican vaquero and a Union veteran in a Western setting."* You'll find that authenticity doesn't mean sameness—it means specificity.

Originality lives in *perspective*. Most Westerns are told from the viewpoint of rugged men with tragic pasts. Try flipping it. Tell your story through the eyes of a child. Or a Native woman. Or a Black doctor trying to build a life in a town that sees him as a threat. Prompt: *"Give me five unique character perspectives for a Western drama that aren't typically seen in classic Westerns."* You'll discover stories waiting in the shadows of history.

Authenticity also comes from emotional truth. The frontier was brutal. Life was uncertain. Grief, hope, fear, and pride were daily companions. Your story becomes more authentic when your characters *feel* real, regardless of their time period. Use ChatGPT to help explore these inner lives: *"What emotional struggles might a widowed rancher face after years of drought and debt?"* That gives you something deeper than costume drama. That gives you humanity.

If you're worried your plot feels familiar, test it. Ask: *"What are five common Western plots, and how can I twist each one to feel new?"* Take "A stranger rides into town." Maybe the stranger is a child. Maybe he's dying. Maybe he's been there before, but no one remembers. These small changes breathe new life into familiar bones.

One excellent way to stay original is through *symbolism*. The West was full of symbols: open land, rising smoke, circling vultures, a lone horse without a rider. Use these, but make them your own. A wedding ring buried in the dirt. A bible with pages missing. A windmill that only turns when someone lies. Ask: *"Suggest original symbolic elements for a Western story about betrayal."* Now your story starts speaking in images, not just words.

Pacing also plays a role in tone. Traditional Westerns often move slow and steady. Try flipping that. What happens when your Western is fast-paced, full of momentum and sudden turns? Or make it introspective, dreamlike, even philosophical. Prompt ChatGPT: *"How can I write a Western with a surreal, poetic tone while keeping the setting grounded?"* You'll get ideas that help you blend the real and the strange.

Authenticity doesn't just live in historical accuracy—it lives in *consistency*. If your world feels real, readers will follow you anywhere. You can even introduce speculative elements—a town with no clocks, a man who never ages—if everything else holds true. Western horror, Western mystery, Western sci-fi—they all work as long as the rules of your world are respected. Ask: *"How can I introduce a supernatural element into a Western without losing authenticity?"* That opens a whole new frontier.

You don't have to choose between honoring the Western and reinventing it.

You can do both—at the same time.

Let your boots walk the dust of truth,

but let your story blaze its own trail through the canyon.

Because the West wasn't made by people who followed a script.

It was built by those who wrote their own—with grit, guts, and something original in their saddlebags.

One Day, One Western: Putting It All Together

You've made it through every piece of the process—idea generation, structure, characters, themes, pacing, twists, dialogue, and that gritty Western voice. You've explored the wind-swept plains of memory, the dirt roads of tragedy, and the hidden springs of redemption. You've seen how ChatGPT can act like a ghost-writer, a scene doctor, a dialogue partner, a structural engineer, and even a mythmaker. Now we ride into the final chapter, the big question: *Can you write a full Western story in one day?* The answer is yes—if you've done the prep, set your pace, and trust the trail.

One day doesn't mean rushing. It means *focusing*. A full Western story, whether short novel, screenplay, or novella, isn't about how many words you write—it's about whether each scene earns its place. And with ChatGPT at your side, you're never writing alone. You're collaborating with a tireless, idea-churning engine that never runs out of dust, drama, or dialogue. You're not just typing—you're building. Fast. With intention.

Here's how to start: wake up with a rough idea of your ending. That's your North Star. Maybe it's the gunslinger walking into the sunset. Maybe it's the sheriff dying with his badge in the dirt. Maybe it's the outlaw realizing the treasure was never gold—it was peace. The end helps you steer every choice. Prompt ChatGPT: *"Give me three possible endings for a Western about a bounty hunter chasing his former mentor."* Choose the one that makes your heart clench. That's your story's soul.

Once you've got your end, backtrack fast. Ask: *"Give me a three-act Western plot outline that leads to this ending."* You'll get the structure: Act One introduces the world and the wound, Act Two deepens the tension and raises the stakes, and Act Three explodes into climax and resolution. Even a tight outline is enough to start riding.

Now it's time to shape your characters. Use the "one line rule." Who is the protagonist, in one sharp sentence? *A preacher who lost his faith but can't stop protecting people. A drifter who once was a killer, now trying not to be.* Ask ChatGPT: *"Develop a character profile for a Western drifter with a dark past but a strict moral code."* Now give them a name, a flaw, a goal—and one person they love or fear.

Every scene you write should have purpose. Don't stop for fluff. Don't meander unless the wandering reveals something real. You can prompt: *"Write the opening scene where the hero rides into a suspicious town."* Then: *"Write the saloon scene where they're warned to leave."* Each prompt builds momentum. And the more you write, the more ChatGPT learns your tone and rhythm. You'll stop prompting full scenes and start shaping faster: *"Give me five different ways to have a tense standoff without immediate violence."*

When you hit dialogue, don't sweat perfection. Use: *"Rewrite this exchange to show tension using subtext."* Or: *"Make this line sound like an 1880s cowboy with a poetic edge."* You keep your style, but you sharpen it, polish it, make it hit harder.

If your story slows down or feels too clean, toss a twist in. Prompt: *"What's a betrayal that could happen in the middle of this story to raise the stakes?"* If your character is growing stale, ask: *"What secret could be revealed that changes how others see the protagonist?"* Plot twists don't have to be huge—they just need to turn the emotional wheel a few notches.

Every few chapters, pause and check your arc. Ask: *"Does this character's journey reflect a deeper emotional transformation?"* If not, rewrite that moment. Use: *"Insert a small scene where the character shows internal change without saying a word."* These little shifts build your Western into something memorable.

And don't forget the land. The setting isn't background—it's breath. Every act should have a visual tone. You can keep the pace fast, but don't sacrifice the dirt and wind and stars. Ask: *"Describe a Western town on the edge of dusk, full of secrets."* That's your atmosphere, your backdrop, your silent witness.

By the time you hit your final scene, you'll know what needs to be said—and what doesn't. Let ChatGPT help you brainstorm endings that *echo* the beginning. A line repeated with new meaning. A gesture carried through. A name finally spoken. Ask: *"Write a Western ending that closes the loop with emotional weight."* Then rewrite it. Refine it. Until it doesn't just end the story—it *finishes* it.

Writing a Western in one day with ChatGPT doesn't mean cheating the process. It means compressing it. Condensing your instinct, your style, your intention—and letting AI be the extra set of hands that helps you stack the bricks faster. You still steer the wagon. You still decide the stakes. But now, you've got a partner riding beside you, ready to answer any question, shape any twist, and fill in any blank.

One day. One story.

No outline? No problem.

No time? You've got just enough.

No excuses. Just grit, speed, and the willingness to ride hard.

Because this isn't just about writing fast.

It's about writing *real.*

And when you put it all together—idea, structure, characters, dialogue, tension, setting, emotion—you won't just have a draft.

You'll have a *Western.*

And by nightfall, you'll have one more thing:

The proof that if you can do this in one day, you can do *anything.*

Examples of Good Prompts for Western Story Design and Structure

You've got the boots on the ground, the sun at your back, and maybe even a character or two walking the streets of your dusty imagination. But the magic of working with ChatGPT to write a Western story—whether it's a screenplay, a novel, a short story, or a TV pilot—starts with knowing how to ask the *right* questions. The better your prompts, the better your answers. A good prompt isn't just a command—it's a conversation starter with your AI partner. It narrows the focus, sets the tone, and invites discovery.

This chapter gives you a range of carefully crafted prompts you can use to build your Western from the ground up—starting with worldbuilding, character design, and conflict, and moving through structure, themes, dialogue, pacing, and revision. These prompts aren't just useful—they're powerful tools to unlock ideas and keep you writing.

1. Conceptualizing the Core Idea

- *"Give me five unique Western story concepts that haven't been done before."*
- *"Pitch me a Western drama where the protagonist isn't a gunslinger or lawman."*
- *"What would a Western story look like if it took place during the winter in Alaska in the 1890s?"*
- *"Design a Western story that focuses on a forgotten town with a cursed reputation."*

2. Designing Your Protagonist

- *"Create a Western protagonist who is haunted by a secret and avoids violence at all costs."*
- *"Describe a female outlaw in a Western setting who has a moral code but is hunted by the law."*
- *"What psychological trauma might drive a retired gunslinger to pick up his weapon again?"*
- *"Write a character profile for a drifter who arrives in town with a hidden motive."*

3. Exploring Supporting Characters

- *"Describe five compelling side characters for a small Western town, each with a dark past."*
- *"Who might be the reluctant deputy to a crooked sheriff?"*
- *"Design a mentor figure for a young outlaw who wants revenge."*
- *"Create an antagonist who thinks they're the hero in a Western."*

4. Creating the Setting and Atmosphere

- *"Build a vivid Western town with 300 residents, a history of violence, and secrets buried in the mine."*
- *"Describe a remote frontier ranch surrounded by land disputes and superstition."*
- *"Give me sensory details for a Western story set in the middle of a desert dust storm."*
- *"What unique traditions or rituals might exist in an isolated mountain town in 1877?"*

5. Plotting with Structure

- *"Give me a three-act structure for a Western revenge story with a tragic ending."*
- *"Outline a Western story in five major beats: intro, conflict, escalation, climax, and resolution."*
- *"What plot twist could shift the midpoint of a Western from a personal journey to a town-wide crisis?"*

- *"Design the key turning point in a Western where the protagonist must choose between justice and loyalty."*

6. Building Tension and Conflict

- *"Write a tense Western scene where two former friends face off without drawing their guns."*
- *"List internal and external conflicts for a rancher trying to protect his land from a railroad company."*
- *"What are different ways a Western character might try to resolve conflict without violence?"*
- *"Describe a moral dilemma faced by a bounty hunter who discovers his target is innocent."*

7. Dialogue and Voice

- *"Write Western-style dialogue between a seasoned outlaw and a teenage boy trying to prove himself."*
- *"Give me five ways a tough frontier woman might express affection without saying 'I love you.'"*
- *"How might a dying lawman deliver a poetic final line?"*
- *"Rewrite this modern dialogue into authentic-sounding Western language."*

8. Themes and Symbolism

- *"Explore the theme of redemption in a Western where the hero has killed someone they loved."*
- *"What symbols can represent guilt, revenge, and justice in a Western setting?"*
- *"Write a Western story centered around the theme 'freedom has a price.'"*
- *"Describe how the landscape can reflect the emotional state of a character in a Western."*

9. Starting and Ending Strong

- *"Write a compelling opening paragraph for a Western story that immediately sets the tone."*
- *"List ways to open a Western novel that feel fresh and mysterious."*
- *"Give me three emotionally powerful Western endings that don't involve violence."*
- *"How can I close a Western story with a symbolic gesture rather than a final gunfight?"*

10. Rewriting and Editing with Style

- *"Rewrite this Western scene to sound more poetic and evocative, using natural imagery."*
- *"Tighten the pacing of this saloon confrontation without losing suspense."*
- *"Can you simplify this paragraph while keeping the Western tone?"*
- *"How can I show rather than tell a character's regret in this moment?"*

These prompts don't just get your story rolling—they help you refine it, deepen it, and push it past cliché. Use them like tools in your saddlebag. When the trail gets hard, when the dust settles in your imagination, reach for a prompt. Adjust it, twist it, and make it yours.

Because the West was built by asking questions. Where's the gold? Where's the danger? Who can I trust? And with ChatGPT, your questions turn into *story*. One prompt at a time, you shape the silence into something unforgettable.

Examples of Good Prompts for Designing Compelling Characters

No Western story is worth a damn without unforgettable characters. You can have a great setting, a solid plot, even a twist that hits like a bolt from the blue—but if your characters don't breathe, bleed, and ride like real people, your story will fall flat. The West was built by wanderers, survivors, dreamers, killers, lovers, and lawmen. It's a land of contradictions, where the hero can be a liar and the villain might be the only one telling the truth. Designing characters for a Western drama means giving them flaws, purpose, and emotional depth. And with ChatGPT in your saddlebag, crafting those characters becomes faster, richer, and infinitely more layered—if you ask the right questions.

The key to a great prompt is specificity. Don't just ask for "a cowboy character." Ask for a *cowboy with a scar on his soul and a secret he'll never speak aloud.* Ask for a *preacher who's lost his faith but keeps preaching because the town needs him to.* The more focused your prompt, the more original your character becomes. Here are the kinds of prompts that can help you create Western characters that linger long after the last page.

1. Basic Character Design

- *"Create a Western protagonist who is brave on the outside but secretly broken inside."*
- *"Design a female outlaw who uses charm and trickery more than guns to get what she wants."*
- *"Write a character profile for a lawman who has never fired his gun and is terrified of the day he will."*
- *"Describe an aging gunslinger who trains a young deputy but fears he's teaching him the wrong lessons."*

2. Character Backstory and Wounds

- *"What tragic event from childhood shaped this cowboy's fear of commitment?"*
- *"Give me a backstory for a saloon owner who used to be a respected doctor."*
- *"Why did this quiet rancher abandon his family years ago—and why is he coming back now?"*
- *"Write a monologue from a bounty hunter who's haunted by the one man he let live."*

3. Motivation and Purpose

- *"What does a former Confederate soldier want more than anything, and what's stopping him from getting it?"*
- *"Describe a character driven by revenge but afraid of who they'll become if they succeed."*
- *"Give me five emotional motivations for a Western character who refuses to speak about their past."*
- *"What could motivate a saloon girl to betray someone she loves?"*

4. Flaws and Contradictions

- *"Design a Western hero whose greatest strength is also their biggest weakness."*
- *"Create a villain who believes they're the only one holding the town together."*
- *"Describe a preacher who secretly gambles, drinks, and doubts the very God he speaks for."*
- *"What does a loyal ranch hand do when the landowner turns out to be the villain?"*

5. Physical and Visual Details

- *"What physical scars tell a story about this character's violent past?"*

- *"Describe a Western character's wardrobe and what it reveals about them emotionally."*
- *"What small, repetitive habit reveals this gunfighter's anxiety?"*
- *"Create a list of personal items this character carries in their saddlebag—and what each item means to them."*

6. Dialogue and Voice

- *"Write dialogue in the voice of a gruff cattleman who refuses to admit he's lonely."*
- *"How would a well-educated but bitter land baron speak to someone he sees as beneath him?"*
- *"What are five catchphrases or expressions this character uses that hint at their trauma?"*
- *"Give me a tense conversation between a woman running from her past and a man who recognizes her."*

7. Relationships and Dynamics

- *"Describe the relationship between an old outlaw and the sheriff who was once his partner."*
- *"What's the dynamic between a father and daughter trying to rebuild their relationship on the frontier?"*
- *"Write a scene where a former best friend returns as an enemy."*
- *"Design a slow-burn romance between a grieving widow and the stranger who saved her son."*

8. Arcs and Transformation

- *"What emotional arc does a bitter bounty hunter experience when he's forced to protect a child?"*
- *"Describe how a naive settler turns into a hardened survivor over the course of the story."*
- *"What is the moment of emotional breaking for a stoic character—and what causes it?"*
- *"How does a villain begin to question everything they've built their life around?"*

9. Unusual and Fresh Characters

- *"Create a Western character who doesn't carry a weapon but is feared anyway."*
- *"Design a mute stable boy who witnesses a murder and knows who's guilty."*
- *"What role does a traveling undertaker play in uncovering secrets across different towns?"*
- *"Write about a woman pretending to be a man to escape her past—and what happens when someone figures it out."*

10. Character Conflicts and Internal Battles

- *"What are five things this character says they believe—and one thing they truly believe deep down?"*
- *"Create an inner monologue of a character wrestling with guilt after killing someone they once admired."*
- *"Write about a character torn between loyalty to their blood family and their found family."*
- *"What are this character's greatest fears—and how do they show those fears without ever saying them out loud?"*

With these prompts, you're not just building personalities—you're building hearts, histories, and whole lives. ChatGPT can help you generate character sheets, test scenes, inner monologues, even full arcs. The more you prompt, the more your character sharpens from silhouette to flesh and blood.

So don't just write about the man with the gun.

Write about why he never draws unless he's shaking.

Don't just write about the woman on the horse.

Write about the wound she carries and the hope she hides.

The West doesn't care how many notches are on your belt.

But your readers will care how deep your characters run.

And it all starts with the right question.

The right prompt. And the willingness to ride deeper.

Examples of Good Prompts for World Building

A Western doesn't just happen on the page—it rises from the dirt, rolls in with the wind, and spreads like wildfire across a reader's imagination. World building in a Western drama means creating more than dusty streets and lonely trails. It's about building a world that feels lived-in, dangerous, romantic, harsh, and sometimes eerily quiet. It's about history under every boot-print, secrets in every canyon, and rules no one dares to write down but everyone knows. When you're building your world with ChatGPT, the key is to focus on details that bring out character, atmosphere, conflict, and emotional tone.

Below are high-impact, genre-specific prompts to help you build an immersive Western world—one fencepost, one bullet hole, one ghost town at a time.

1. Starting with the Town or Settlement

- *"Describe a Western frontier town built around a failed gold mine—include geography, architecture, and population."*
- *"Create a town that looks respectable on the surface but hides criminal operations underground."*
- *"Give me five unique small Western towns, each defined by a single dominant trade or secret."*
- *"Describe a town where the sheriff, doctor, and preacher all have something to hide from one another."*

2. Environment and Geography

- *"Build a Western setting in a canyon region where water is sacred and rare."*
- *"Describe the landscape of a high desert plateau town on the brink of drought."*
- *"Give me five types of frontier environments that could shape the characters who live there."*
- *"Create a description of a prairie settlement constantly threatened by blizzards and wolves."*

3. Daily Life and Culture

- *"Describe the daily routines of a small Western town, from sunrise to sunset."*
- *"What kind of entertainment, traditions, and taboos might exist in a town built around a railroad station?"*
- *"List ten details that show how people live, survive, and celebrate in an 1880s frontier town."*
- *"Describe the social hierarchy in a cattle town where ranchers, cowhands, and townsfolk coexist uneasily."*

4. Law, Order, and Power Structures

- *"Explain how justice is handled in a Western town that has no formal court system."*
- *"Describe the dynamic between a mining company that owns the land and a sheriff who resents them."*
- *"What happens in a Western town when the sheriff disappears and the town must govern itself?"*
- *"Create a list of unofficial rules the townspeople follow in a place with a violent history."*

5. Technology and Infrastructure

- *"What kinds of technology would exist in an 1870s Western rail town?"*
- *"Describe how a telegraph station operates in a remote settlement and who controls it."*

- *"List five important locations in a Western town and how they operate—blacksmith, church, saloon, jail, and schoolhouse."*
- *"How does a lack of communication affect the lives of people living in a Western town surrounded by wilderness?"*

6. Politics and Tension

- *"Describe a Western town caught between two rival landowners vying for control."*
- *"How would a Western town deal with settlers from different backgrounds clashing over land, language, and law?"*
- *"Create a political tension between railroad expansionists and traditional cattle ranchers."*
- *"What power struggles might occur in a Western town where a preacher, a saloon owner, and a mayor all want influence?"*

7. Mysticism, Folklore, and Local Legends

- *"Invent a ghost story locals in a mining town believe—and how it affects their behavior."*
- *"Describe superstitions and myths believed by residents of an isolated Western canyon village."*
- *"Create a Western town where people believe in omens from animals and the changing winds."*
- *"What old folk tale keeps children indoors after sundown in a frontier town surrounded by woods?"*

8. History and Backstory

- *"What event in this town's past still shapes its laws and superstitions today?"*
- *"Describe a forgotten massacre that the town never talks about—but that everyone remembers."*
- *"What year was this town founded, by whom, and why—and what was left behind to rot?"*
- *"Build a timeline of major events in a Western settlement that grew too fast and fell too hard."*

9. Trade, Survival, and Economy

- *"What kind of economy would develop in a remote town with no railroad and dangerous trade routes?"*
- *"How would a frontier town based around a silver mine change once the silver ran out?"*
- *"Describe the barter system in a struggling town during a harsh winter."*
- *"List ten professions in a Western town and what kind of people hold those jobs."*

10. Unique Town Features and Unusual World Elements

- *"Invent a Western town built inside the crater of an ancient meteorite, and describe how it affects life there."*
- *"Describe a saloon that's also a courthouse, run by a judge who drinks on the job."*
- *"What makes this Western town famous—or infamous—across the region?"*
- *"Build a Western town near sacred Native land, where ancient boundaries are crossed in secret."*

These prompts aren't just about painting pretty scenery. They help you discover the *culture* of your world—its fears, routines, rules, and whispers. You're not just writing about buildings and roads. You're writing about people who built those things with blood and hope, and who are trying to survive under skies that don't always forgive.

The more specific you are in your prompts, the more alive your world becomes.

The more alive your world is, the more real your characters feel.

And the more real your characters feel,

the more unforgettable your story becomes.

Examples of Good Prompts for Western Story Ideas

Every great Western starts with a spark—one image, one moment, one question that lights a fire and kicks up the dust. It could be a man walking into town with no name and a bullet scar beneath his collar. A woman digging a grave outside a burned-down church. A boy who sees something in the desert no one believes. The idea doesn't have to be complicated—it just has to *hook you*. It should feel like it's already galloping through your imagination, waiting for you to saddle up and chase it down.

When you're using ChatGPT to generate story ideas for a Western, the trick is to ask prompts that are part image, part emotion, and part conflict. A good story idea prompt invites characters, setting, danger, and theme to ride together. Below is a list of high-quality prompts—ready to inspire the next dusty showdown, desperate chase, or quiet moment that changes everything.

1. Classic Story Idea Prompts with a Twist

- *"Give me five Western story ideas that begin with a stranger riding into town and end with a secret buried."*
- *"Write a Western story idea where the outlaw is actually the only honest person in town."*
- *"Give me a Western revenge story where the hero chooses mercy—and pays the price."*
- *"What's a Western story where the sheriff is protecting the wrong people?"*

2. Character-Driven Story Prompts

- *"Create a Western story idea about a preacher who loses his faith and becomes a bounty hunter."*
- *"Give me a story idea where a young woman disguises herself as a man to join a wagon train and find her missing brother."*
- *"Write a Western plot centered on a Native American tracker caught between two cultures."*
- *"Describe a Western story where a lawman hunts down his own son, who's turned outlaw."*

3. Plot-Driven Ideas Built Around Conflict

- *"What's a story idea involving two rival ranchers whose children fall in love?"*
- *"Give me a Western mystery about a town where people keep vanishing into the hills."*
- *"Describe a Western heist story where the target is not gold, but a wanted prisoner."*
- *"Write a Western about a town that burns down—and the survivors trying to rebuild while hunted by the same men who destroyed it."*

4. Theme-Based Western Story Prompts

- *"What's a Western story built around the theme of redemption after betrayal?"*
- *"Create a story idea exploring the cost of loyalty between two former outlaws."*
- *"Give me a Western plot where the theme is justice versus survival."*
- *"Write a Western drama where the real antagonist is time—running out, catching up, or being lost forever."*

5. Genre-Bending Western Ideas

- *"Combine the Western genre with Gothic horror—what kind of story could emerge?"*
- *"Create a Western story that includes speculative science fiction but stays grounded in character."*
- *"What's a supernatural Western involving a ghost town where the dead whisper warnings?"*
- *"Describe a Western noir set in a border town full of secrets and double-crosses."*

6. Setting-Based Story Starters

- *"Write a story set entirely during a three-day blizzard in a remote Western fort."*
- *"What happens when a Western town runs out of water, and the nearest river is claimed by someone dangerous?"*
- *"Create a plot based on a stagecoach stuck halfway between two towns—where everyone aboard has a secret."*
- *"Describe a Western set in a dying mining camp where the workers strike back against the owners."*

7. Unusual Character Combinations

- *"Give me a Western story where a pacifist doctor is forced to protect a violent fugitive."*
- *"Write a story idea featuring an ex-slave turned cattle baron and a Pinkerton agent sent to spy on him."*
- *"Describe a Western where a child and an aging outlaw travel together after escaping a massacre."*
- *"What story could come from a wandering piano player who knows a secret that could destroy a town?"*

8. High Stakes & Ticking Clocks

- *"Create a Western story that takes place over 24 hours during a town's annual festival—while a robbery is being planned."*
- *"Write a story idea where a train is hijacked, and the passengers must figure out who's behind it before it reaches the canyon."*
- *"Describe a Western built around a cattle drive gone wrong, with food running out and a killer among the crew."*
- *"What's a story idea where the protagonist has three days to cross outlaw territory to deliver a message that could prevent war?"*

9. Morally Complex Story Ideas

- *"What's a story where the hero is hired to protect land that was stolen from someone else?"*
- *"Describe a Western drama where the protagonist must choose between saving a town or saving their child."*
- *"Write a story idea about an outlaw who is offered a pardon in exchange for hunting down his own gang."*
- *"Give me a plot where two former best friends are on opposite sides of a range war, neither one fully right or wrong."*

10. Story Ideas that End with a Question

- *"Create a Western that ends with the hero walking away—not because he won, but because he couldn't afford to lose again."*
- *"What's a story that ends with the villain escaping and the hero questioning everything they stood for?"*
- *"Write a Western where the final scene leaves the reader unsure who was telling the truth all along."*
- *"Describe a Western story that ends with peace—but at a price no one expected."*

These prompts are your flint and steel.

Each one is a chance to light a fire under your imagination and see where the smoke leads.

The West is wide. The possibilities are endless.

And all it takes is one good question—

one good *start*— to begin the ride of your life.

Your One-Day Western Writing Game Plan – From Start to Publish

So you've got one day to write and publish a full Western story. Sounds impossible? It's not. With ChatGPT as your partner and a clear, no-nonsense game plan, you can turn dust into gold in 24 hours or less. Whether you're writing a short story, novella, or even a screenplay, the key is clarity, speed, and creative momentum. No backtracking. No overthinking. Just saddle up, ride hard, and don't stop until the story's told.

Here's your hour-by-hour guide to going from blank page to published piece—with your hat still on straight.

Hour 1: Lock the Core Idea and Ending

Start with your foundation. You don't need to know everything yet—just the bones. Use ChatGPT to help brainstorm:

"Give me five original Western story ideas with emotional depth."

Pick the one that punches you in the gut or makes your chest tighten. Now jump to the end.

Ask: *"How could this story end in a powerful, poetic, or tragic way?"*

Choose the ending that matters. You now know where you're riding to.

Hour 2: Map Out a Rough Three-Act Structure

With your idea and ending in hand, use:

"Create a three-act structure for this Western idea."

Refine it with a few follow-ups if needed. Act One introduces the world and wound. Act Two complicates everything. Act Three delivers the showdown and resolution. This isn't a screenplay beat sheet—it's a rough trail map.

Hour 3: Flesh Out the Main Character(s)

Now you need your lead—someone the reader will ride with to the end. Ask:

"Create a Western protagonist with a complex backstory and strong internal conflict."

Then:

"Write a short character profile for the main antagonist, with believable motivation."

You can also generate side characters as needed: the deputy, the barkeep, the preacher, the outlaw's son.

Hour 4: Open With Impact

Ask ChatGPT:

"Write the first 300 words of a Western story where the protagonist arrives in a hostile town."

Then edit it until it feels like *you.* This is your voice. Your style. You're not just starting the story—you're establishing the tone, the stakes, and the mood.

Hours 5–9: Write the Full Draft, Scene by Scene

You've got five hours to ride the length of the story. Break it into scenes and write each one using focused prompts like:

- *"Write a scene where the hero first meets the antagonist, and tension builds."*
- *"Write a flashback revealing the protagonist's greatest regret."*
- *"Write a Western action scene where the hero and sidekick ambush a gang."*

Use ChatGPT for fast dialogue, sensory description, or rough drafts of emotional moments. Paste your lines in, ask for punch-ups, get suggestions, and move forward.

Finish each scene and move on. Don't linger. Don't edit yet. Just ride.

Hour 10: The Final Showdown and Resolution

Now, write the final confrontation. Ask:

"Write a climactic Western scene where the hero must choose between vengeance and mercy."

Then write the aftermath. Use a prompt like:

"Write the closing paragraph of a Western story that leaves the reader emotionally satisfied but haunted."

Close the loop. Deliver what you promised in the opening. Stick the landing.

Hour 11: Editing, Trimming, and Polishing

Now you edit. Use prompts like:

- *"Tighten this scene and remove unnecessary lines."*
- *"Make this dialogue sharper and more Western in tone."*
- *"How can I improve the pacing of this chapter?"*

Clean up your structure. Smooth transitions. Strengthen your voice.

Hour 12: Format and Publish

You've got a finished draft. Now it's time to share it.

If it's a short story or novella, format it in Word or Google Docs, save as PDF, and upload to Amazon KDP, Draft2Digital or Wattpad. Use a prompt like:

"Create a short description and genre tags for a Western novella about a grieving sheriff hunting his former mentor."

Need a quick cover? Ask ChatGPT to help you prompt an image generator:

"Generate a prompt for an AI image of a lone cowboy riding toward a blood-red sunset."

Upload it. Add your title. Hit publish.

By sunset, here's what you've done:

- Conceptualized a complete, emotionally resonant Western story
- Designed compelling characters with clear arcs
- Written a full draft scene by scene, using AI to keep momentum
- Revised and polished with precision prompts
- Formatted, packaged, and published your finished work

You didn't wait for inspiration.

You didn't wander the desert of doubt.

You saddled up, pointed your story toward the horizon, and *rode it to the end.*

That's what writing in one day is about.

It's not about being perfect.

It's about finishing the damn ride.

And with ChatGPT in your corner,

you never had to do it alone.

I hope you found inspiration within these pages. If you liked this book, please leave a review where you bought it. Thank you from the author.

www.ingramcontent.com/pod-product-compliance
Lightning Source LLC
LaVergne TN
LVHW082348200926
848481LV00012B/3491